Indebted to Change

Indebted to Change

The Beggar Poet's I Ching

Stephen Falconer

RESOURCE *Publications* · Eugene, Oregon

INDEBTED TO CHANGE
The Beggar Poet's I Ching

Copyright © 2021 Stephen Falconer. All rights reserved. Except for brief quotations in critical publications or reviews, no part of this book may be reproduced in any manner without prior written permission from the publisher. Write: Permissions, Wipf and Stock Publishers, 199 W. 8th Ave., Suite 3, Eugene, OR 97401.

Resource Publications
An Imprint of Wipf and Stock Publishers
199 W. 8th Ave., Suite 3
Eugene, OR 97401

www.wipfandstock.com

PAPERBACK ISBN: 978-1-7252-9831-6
HARDCOVER ISBN: 978-1-7252-9832-3
EBOOK ISBN: 978-1-7252-9833-0

Manufactured in the U.S.A.   04/21/21

Dedicated to Helen

Contents

1. Vocation | 1
2. Homeliness | 6
3. Heartsore | 11
4. Next to Nowhere | 14
5. Waiting for Sunrise | 17
6. Conflict | 24
7. Warfare | 29
8. Commitment | 35
9. On the Brink of Discovery | 39
10. A Warning without Warning | 44
11. Not Far to Go | 48
12. Stagnation | 53
13. A Family of Friends | 58
14. From out of a Stranger's Heart | 63
15. Humility | 69
16. A Kindred Spirit | 73
17. Inner Light | 77
18. Renewal | 81
19. Something You'll Leave Behind | 86
20. From Different Points of View | 93
21. I'll Get to You Somehow | 99
22. Beauty | 104
23. Netherworld | 107
24. Rejuvenation | 110
25. Conscience | 115
26. Clear-headedness | 119
27. Nourishment | 126
28. Overwhelmed | 129
29. Peril | 135
30. Lost in Light | 138
31. Sensitivity | 143
32. Forever | 146
33. Out of Sight | 150
34. Intuition | 153
35. A Warm Heart | 156
36. Gloom | 159
37. A Reason to Remain | 163
38. At Opposite Ends | 166
39. Forgetfulness | 171
40. Release | 175

CONTENTS

41 Diminution | 180
42 Ascension | 185
43 A Legitimate Request | 187
44 A Way Out of Hell | 189
45 A Common Interest | 192
46 As Far as I Can Go | 196
47 Sorrow | 199
48 Wellspring | 204
49 A New Start | 207
50 A Meal for One | 215
51 Shock | 220
52 Quietude | 223

53 Development | 227
54 Vitriol | 233
55 Glory | 237
56 Wayfarer | 242
57 Transcendence | 246
58 Happiness | 253
59 Commiseration | 257
60 A Way Nonetheless | 261
61 Sincerity | 266
62 Hopelessness | 269
63 An Uncertain Future | 272
64 Almost There | 277

1
Vocation

For the fair next week
I'll make a banner telling everyone what I'm up to

(louts hang around under the lamp outside)

how I spend two or three hours a day

(should I hear their chatter crackling like wildfire
I'll hit the wall).

The script will not only depict my credentials,
but be written
with attention to how form embellishes meaning:

The Beggar Poet—

in black with a blue border—

for all occasions, easy
to anger, quick to take offence,
who'll write of anything you'll put before him

alive
to tradition,
one of many

solitary enough to contemplate a kindred spirit
who could tell
just by looking at the sea
whether a storm will ensue:

"dark flecks on the swell,
a seagull afraid to settle"

the latest text which aims to find the spring
at the center:

"Exit

Obliterating the instinct for survival
or yearning for being an entity,
a whisper named conscience
disappearing to the extreme limit with no return
or memory
of having been posited by a self-assured skull,
ending ownership of insight

without seeing
or hearing,
facing toward faceless being

1: VOCATION

a way
to nullify the wan glow,
demean 'achievement'

blank out,
expire

out of light"

late for meditation,
a bald monk who'd observe interesting items
even though it means missing the late-night duty
of sweeping crumbs
from the floor:

her pale skin
and white umbrella, absence of chatter
as she watches raindrops darken incense ash

a tooth missing, an earring made of bone

coils springing from the chair offered for sale,
the certainty it will outlast any rump
that has the pleasure to sit on it

ice cubes used to keep silver fish cold,
each eye's dead stare
cold as the bottom of the sea

a grasshopper flitting from a rusted can
to a splash of midday on pumpkin rind,
the heartbeat still seeking its mate
in the space between one leap
and another

a sparrow's nest,
speckled, tiny eggs

the weight
of devotion and warmth, finally
a crack letting the sun come in

(I'll move to another corner
If the ruckus persists,
the attempt to draw another character's put off)

nothing can disrupt power to exist:

an ant carrying a load larger than its body,
a swallow diving to protect her nest

the pressure of centuries lived
and unlived in,
an inkling I'll get by on oats and water
for the rest of my life

the moon's rise and sun's glare,
in the middle counting the hours
before they change places

softening the edges,
hardening the center, rolling off the end

WHO'LL

coaxing light into ink,
distinguishing a break and the beginning

LISTEN

left, upwards or right

WITH

an incoming sweep,
return heavenwards

AN OPEN EYE

this way.

2

Homeliness

Without fail, once a year,
the madame who owns the gaudy parlor
on the edge of town
invites me to celebrate the family tree
which she and I, albeit indirectly, are connected to.

Making it worthwhile
is the tasty soup she provides,
although it is customary to repay her kindness
by painting a bench, mending a chair
or, for the less enthusiastic,
sweeping leaves from the path.

Kneeling before the tiny altar
she has erected in the garden,
it is incumbent upon me
to reflect on the providence
that has brought us to share
in afternoon companionship

yet, in the valley,
where wind erodes the heights
and the scent of ant, worm
and leaf mold reaches the clouds,
the tears of a retainer bound in servitude
to one he adored.

2: HOMELINESS

I'll be the shadow crossing the graveyard
or the mellow glow from an oil lamp:

when every pill had been chewed and swallowed,
he boiled herbs in a mixture
that would,
if the proportions were correct,
revive her mood and alleviate her pain

at the end of a long year,
placed flowers on her tomb,
collected a handful
of dust
and allowed it to scatter
where cloud shadows rest upon a meadow

deserted burrows letting in moonlight,
red ants retreating to a cleft

an era befriended by otherworldly calling
just outside the limit
of perception . . .

someday,
to build into a block used to reach the apex
of fortification looking down upon a friend
and an intruder:

as they walked by the bamboo grove,
he offered to carry her satchel,
blew kisses

on her wedding night,
settled her youngsters into an afternoon nap

when dew froze on the bough,
put a match to tinder
in the hearth,
warming their joints and knuckles

touched her lips—

cold,
with the dread of incoming horsemen.

Against her breast
a portrait
of the mother who forbade illicit glances
toward the dark hearted passing by:

an emperor's desire to invade regions
where he hadn't been invited—

the glazed bowl upended,
chunks of apple and pepper stuck to the ceiling—

illuminate the interior,
discover heretofore unknown depths:

"heavy dew's a suitable ingredient
for love,
uncured flesh the remedy for heartache"

in the limb that deflected the blow
that ended her breathing—

blue mingling white and black:

a moist wick that sputters
and hardly distinguishes the narrow entrance,
an earthenware pot full
to the brim

moisture from wasteland flower heads,
scent that befits someone
who'd recall forgotten dynasties and unmemorable eons
before the earth withdrew from the sun

droplets moistening layers of dust
and leaving every particle touching the other
with the same stuff
that fell only a moment before.

From the height of his century,
he would,
If he could,
have reaffirmed life in her bones,
fire in her blood,
the surge and flow of bodily fluid

the pulse and murmuring heart

caught the wind
and filled her lungs,
brushed the soil on her lips
away with a finger,
straightened the bow in her back
by a gentle tug at each end.

With the deftness of one used to preparing a meal
for twenty kin
and the neighbors,
she'll set the container back on its base,
pour in sun warmed fruit
and ice water,
shred green leaves until the juice stains her fingertips

let the ingredients simmer
until every mouth can taste the flame
that rises
without burning,
carefully spoon the contents
into the last person's dish:

an ageing poet,
who offered to help with mundane chores,
waiting to be served.

3

Heartsore

If you deliver a box of fruit to the neighbors,
make sure you step by,
for I haven't seen you
since the first night
when you sheltered from the storm.

Would you remember the songs
we shared?

Amongst the bramble
yellow flowers, in the clouds
a hint
of blue,
in the hedgerow red
and absence of motion before the rain came down.

A minstrel plucking a bow
fast as an oarsman pulling against the tide,
tears springing from a drunkard
after a night
without Heaven's assent,
the sodden garments
of a traveler who couldn't stop
for fear he'd miss entry into the pass
before mud
and stones prevented access.

3: HEARTSORE

Light on the door,
a glow through the hall,
over the frame
illumination,
glare on a junk before the thunder sounds

I'll give my all.

A curse losing way from antiquity,
drummers hitting the palate
of a man bent on his knees,
the violet dove fluttering where dreams are erased.

Moist air between the sheets,
someone
who'll love when the flood recedes,
a gentle settling on the attempt
to strike a match
when the lights go out.

A ghost who swallows her children,
descent from higher forms scented
with night . . .

before the mood shifted,
my eyes became clearer
and I could construct a line
with no compulsion to impress
with meaning

instead,
responding to the images you evoked
and finishing the flask
on the table:

toward morning unto evening,
hold back the ache
that could drench my cheeks

the corner
of your eye,
a gasp
for fresh air

a chance to say from the bottom
of my being

somnolent breath
on tired joints

a scratch under your chin,
passers-by entwined

the caress until time to go

how much you mean to me.

4

Next to Nowhere

I could capture fresh air
and hold it
for nights when I close the window
against the frost.

The best way?

I shall ask the spiritual plane

it knows about aether and preservation.

I shall accumulate notes on how to free the passage
before it drives through

ready,
with a bottle in hand,
I'll concentrate, commit to the present

and spring.

4: NEXT TO NOWHERE

The witness
from the hierarchies of Heaven
will address me
at the time
when it is ripe to attack the emptiness,
catch the wind, land lightly
on my feet

transmogrify the past
with the fullness
of absence.

I shall ask the illustrious master
where to store it
if I reach that far.

How indeed?

Erstwhile disposition
to ascend
when luminous beams charge into my spine

gateway into sublime fields:

the cataract that goes upwards
and the fall, unbeknownst
to lower order,
fructifying abeyance of need to be below

clustering vines hanging from gilded windows,
lake in the air,
strolling about dragon's lair, the water
in Heaven

ripe as the custodian
who allows you to enter.

The flame, captivated in inertia,
singeing a goddess's brow,
brightening the milk bubbling in my heart

it has never been done before.

The first thought asked over and again:

Am I doing the right thing?

Ethereality confined to an early riser
awakened
by thunder, allowed to circulate
and return to the source
from which it came.

An answer:

"Stay on the ground."

5

Waiting for Sunrise

Before the moon
can be seen clearly on the wane,
I hope you'll join me
to contemplate
how your old friend muddied the waters
when he discarded reams
of paper, his entire output,
because he couldn't foresee
why anyone would sift through scribblings
he'll never finish
to discover echoes from another era

indecipherable from crow noise,
discolored meat
and blood

a witness,
who'll want to show as soon
as frost congeals in a naked lump
and the cold reaches our dreams,
grass sticks up above the ground.

I expect
you'll turn up,
admonish me for foolishness,

help collect the sodden pages
and dry them over a flame

show where they veer from sanity:

sticky stuff
on her cheek, the smell
of salt as she fended off a suitor from the north

against a grey sky
lumps of feathers,
black throats and bad language

a lean horse spurred on
to the hills,
mindful of return

a curse
for not looking after the first born,
spit in the heart turned to dust.

The evening will sink
in unsweetened air, night linger
in darkness
as if realizing the difficulty changing into daybreak

there never seems an end

5: WAITING FOR SUNRISE

I would, that I could, in one mighty effort,
collapse the labor of years
in a pulse, express each nuance
no matter how deeply embedded
and isolate where every shadow falls
before I can no longer lift a pen

you, on the other hand,
would mark a tree with a notch
where the tide reached its height,
and again
on the rocks where it subsided

every day
check the variations,
observe the center of the extremes
and hold to the shore:

"This is the point
at which I could stand,
knee deep in water,
if need be,
and give thanks to the heavens
for giving me the capacity
to ameliorate the force of imbalance
on my heart."

You'll even accompany my search
in lamplight further downstream:

"Here are some wrapped around the reeds,
but I'm afraid they're illegible

5: WAITING FOR SUNRISE

(the quagmire deeper than anticipated)

you'll have to recollect
what happened
between the malignant call
for revenge
and its repetition down the line."

The inevitable return—

sunken cheekbone,
tang of spent fluid,
drunken gait.

The departure—

dragging to the well to wash,
replacing the broken railings,
checking to see whether the children survived

cold,
sick lips.

When every page has been put
in its rightful place,
we'll trace over the smears
and recollect a few syllables before they disappear:

5: WAITING FOR SUNRISE

gelid trail,
eyestalk, hanging limb

spineless

near,
far, flickering

head
and torso on the move

razor sharp

hooves

mulch,
sap, toadstools

slugs drop

on the ridge

ill in the heart

in her lap

"I'll squash him."

Maybe, with the firelight
in your eyes
and a cup of tea,
the task will near the end:

"Have you recovered the vow she made
never to let go hatred,
season after season,
in expectation he'd appear in the valley
when her breasts were full
and the child ached for comfort?

Will you, however, as I suggest,
remove a dark spot from her quick
and fill the pass with fresh layers

when the thaw enables shoots
to displace hard earth,
notice a bridle twisted around a stump,
a hand wedged between rocks
and a grimace upturned toward the treetops?"

Why not
get in touch with you now?

Because every night cries raise
To Heaven

your mother is injured and must be cared for

I must bide my time

yet,
I know, with your kindness,
warm hands and devotion
to exigencies not of your own making,
it is only a matter of tomorrow
when red edges will creep toward the center

and we can see one another again.

6
Conflict

The water is fresh.

You won't drink
for fear I have contaminated it

still hold a grudge
for my drunken romp through your vegetable patch.

My apology hits the right note.

You won't listen

it reflects the doubt of making sense
of an accusation:

rats in the pipes have everything
to do with the way I walk
and the color of my teeth

reluctant to shake hands, throw away the knives—

6: CONFLICT

an emperor's decree
that forbade trespass upon holy ground?

The crumpled paper you tossed in the weeds
unravels the rhythms of ancient sages.

You will not read it

it doesn't provide a practical solution
how to build an empire on broken bones,
only sounds nonsensical
and misses the point
of getting on in life.

Obvious how much you treasured your onions
when, at dawn,
you ordered your wife outside to water the seedlings

determined to succeed in the local contest
when you made her dig the rows
over
and again

rain or shine

late at night,
for fear of being beaten,
your son would creep between each plant
and attack the creatures that would devour your good work—

reluctant subjects,
who protested against the boundaries
of an all-embracing identity,
summarily tied against a pillar?

on the festival stage
at the day's end, you would look for the scowls
of beaten competitors
and clap your hands
at the murk in their breasts

unidentifiable from the worm that eats into the spine.

"I know how you feel
when I trampled on your precious shoots

it was not my intention
to destroy them

in following the course of the moon
I ended up over the fence,
every second it held still
the glow on my wrist picked out spots
the shape of a sword about to topple a motionless head,
at the instant I discerned a flicker
nothing seemed so pure

all else in shadow:

6: CONFLICT

the journey strangled in mid-flight,
an out-of-this-world keeper tying knots
in blood vessels,
the stamp upon the next earthly plot
indebted to continuity

still again

a vast arena flooded,
entry into the next phase surpassing a twinkle in both eyes
that meant leaping to the harbinger of vision

ears cocked toward applause, a fared nostril."

Should I wrap it in leaves,
place it on your doorstep,
drive it into your heart

but the force of a tyrant will only dispel goodwill,
a sojourn that defies gravity
for a glimpse of unending light
only confute the pleasures of a fellow sufferer

not everyone can breathe rarefied air,
cross swollen rivers,
cohabit realms where the ancients divulge secrets:

"We'll strike
when you least expect"

6: CONFLICT

let it be

take him an onion
you have stored in the cupboard over winter.

7

Warfare

A marrow squashed by an awkward step
and a stick broken
in two—

the shopkeeper's son's mortal wound
and the old lady
who lives at the end of the street's letter
written on foreign soil:

"I have lost a leg,
but look forward to helping in the garden."

Again they demand sacrifice—
another conflict in a land ripe for the taking.

"The unalterable path of a people on the verge
of greatness. Protection of our interests."

I remember my own time obeying orders,
aiming at targets I could hardly see
and handing information to an officer
who, before he lost an eye,
held an outpost no one thought defendable

7: WARFARE

at his disposal
a small group facing the enemy,
including a lad, unbeknownst to his parents,
caught up in warfare echoing the destiny
of his forebears:

a foot soldier
who bit his lower lip.

"Pull yourself together. Are you fit
to hold a weapon?
Are you a coward at heart?"

"Anything but that.
I'll do anything to show
I can stand up to any threat."

The moon's intoxicated surveillance

motion impelling darkness
to eclipse pallid summers, hail
to pelt earthwards, brawn
to spurt eyewards

lighting to crack the skin of night

horns blown
at dawn,
charcoal turned to reveal the glow,
iron pots bubbling over

allowing me—her hands,
breathing,
her whispering:

"I'll give you all"

stakes impaling an ash flecked morning,
silence thick on every tongue

a thousand counts between one
and two,
mulberries staining raw foliage

the distant sea brushed by an eerie squall

scratches across a cheek,
my comrade in arms

the moist lull between earthly odor
and intake of air

knowing your daughter is mine

her traits, her wit,
redoubtable spirit—

the emission
of amorous solicitude

earrings resembling a lioness's claws,
veins entering an enormous cloudbank

hair above her nipple,
the serpent entwining a stump and dozing
as the newly born fieldmouse sleeps in naked folds

that thistle
I plucked between seven
and nine,
I pissed over there

her son spat at me,
the little bastard

broke his collarbone,
kicked him down the stairs

"In Heaven's name
I will stand firm
without flinching

look at your own hand trembling."

A figure pointing toward the sunset:

"Come this way."

7: WARFARE

The translucent door between glowing fields
and the mutilated body left behind on the meadow:

"I'll hold it open for another to follow."

Accompaniment of cymbals over a steady beat,
the warning never to drop one's guard
even though water seems placid,
the day serene
and every flower blooming in colorful array:

"Watch your step."

I hear the moaning as I pass her window,
count the corpses, read about the incursions
into no man's land,
wait until news
of progress has been reported,
finger the bruise on my temple
and resuscitate the same old memorial
interred with the deceased:

there is reason to believe
in attack
as there is meaning in retreat,
a time to take up arms
and a time to lay them down,
but nothing on earth
to assuage the pain
when so many who are barely out of their teens
lose their lives
in a battle that could have been fought

7: WARFARE

by a divine intercessor,
the makers
of weapons

by older officials who put them there.

8
Commitment

I'll invite you to meet me
for tea

we could discuss the levity
with which we bore our grudges,
the palest shade when you splashed paint in landscapes
and I tried to convey how it felt to dance without a partner
on New Year's Eve

whether we will ascend the peak
or delve in the undergrowth.

But do you want to spend time on a veranda
where the supports are giving way,
seats buckle under your weight

the luminous dust you collect
from dreams shaded by unswept leaves,
the gold clasp holding hair
in place awkward
in light filtering through cobwebs?

8: COMMITMENT

We could compose a piece
that brought together your thoughts of Heaven,
"the undifferentiated expanse that precedes the image,"
and my feelings about life

how earth crumbles in your fist
when you squeeze tightly.

But since you devote long hours to vital issues
you may not want to contemplate flecks on the horizon.

I recollect an evening when school had been dismissed
for want of a teacher:

a tireless exercise counting each star,
so,
at the end,
when our fingertips amounted to the same number,
a chariot would fly over the clouds

on the moon's surface
drunk with anticipation
a dragon carry us back to earth.

On festival days,
a choir hit the right tone
when every member concentrated
on the part
they were meant to play
in the swell
and decrease mimicking birds

8: COMMITMENT

in the forest,
a waterfall
and trees with no foliage

keeping the tension alive by pursing our lips,
breathing deeply between our teeth
and swallowing phlegm
before it stuck to our palates.

I can see from the news reports
people of office will be exceptionally busy

but If I don't contact you now
the chance will not come again . . .

I *shall* post the letter ...

we mention the drone
of a bee hovering on a delicate path,
the murmur of assent

blue wisteria

surprise one other remembering what the other didn't:

the cut on my knee climbing over a neighbor's fence
after stealing a plum, conscience

8: COMMITMENT

when you forgot to deliver a thankyou note
to the woman
who helped you find your way home

tears,
when at the end of a long summer, we waved goodbye

laugh over silliness
and folly,
reconstruct childhood dreams

how you wanted to be a poet
and I a man of importance

yet,
with the ebb of the tide,
the waning of the moon
and the unlikely to meet who shared our lives

how you took a position of leadership

while I wandered the streets
in search of something interesting to say
about how I avoided service.

9

On the Brink of Discovery

My reflection

unshaven, blemished,
a droop in one eyelid

hunt a blank sheet
to make notes for a journal:

tonight, I'll

nothing much

prepare supper

sugar granules lost between cracks,
tins piled in a corner,
the tea bag used for the tenth time

imagine I could have been a scholar,
illuminating the ocean
and discovering the deepest creature,

following its path till every secret
of its dark life divulges
why the sword presses against one temple
and not another

however,
as my pen poises an inch above the surface,
the pane cracks—

a flurry of snow
on the path, a rap
on the door, blubbering lips
of the messenger:

"I'm sorry, I've got bad news"

with the cunning
of a transparent shadow,
hiding where every new word
could articulate the meaning of drudgery
and loneliness, a mosquito hovers over my shoulder—

the swell at the mouth of the river,
roar of the waves
and surge against the rocks
where he'd often go to collect shellfish
and sell them at the markets in the city

the misplaced foot
and the plunge,
the scrape against barnacles

9: ON THE BRINK OF DISCOVERY

and the crushing weight dumped
on his back

the smothering taste
of salt
and kelp twisted around ankles,
the snap of a tendon
and the stick through an eyeball—

on the verge of capturing,
I'm sure, why at this time,
in this manner
and for what investiture in poverty,
my father at my birth,
surrendered to an unearthly presence calling on him for release,
the broken window let in a breeze which ruffled the paper—

wind
across my mother's brow raising her forelock,
a loose-fitting gown she wore
on the day my father was placed
in a casket

in the moment
I translated the gibberish
that swims from out of subterranean caverns,
the mosquito needled my ear—

a smack for breaking a plate, the family heirloom:

9: ON THE BRINK OF DISCOVERY

under a plum tree,
wrist dangling in the lake,
ripples
and blue rope mooring a craft to the shore

eyes full of white cloud, the glaze upon an afternoon sun

refusal to swim in the deep side of the river
where it curved around the shallows

how I wouldn't join the others
for fear I'd lose my balance and fall in,
but sat in the pebbles, throwing arcs
of water into the light

a kite flying in the blue sky, held by a small hand,
tugging until disappearing where,
on another occasion far into the future,
I'd be seen on a mountain path

far outside the chatter and mayhem
that at any moment
fine print would appear suspended
in dew

why,
without warning,
a loved one must succumb to a faraway echo
that demands obedience

9: ON THE BRINK OF DISCOVERY

a figure on an upward curve,
who'd just as readily drink darkness from each cloudbank
as brush eyebrows against powered blossom,
close the distance between inertia
and flights that have no boundary
as empty a yawn of all vestiges of ennui

but, as the mist dissolves and I catch a glimpse . . .

late at night, awake and listening to sobbing
that could only come
from one who lost her dearest

be that as it may,
I'll fold the paper in half, scent it with incense
and use it to identify the spot
in my diary where I will explore the abyss,
scan the horizon
where glowing sentinels ask the traveler's identity
as if only I entered their environs

long after the dew washed downstream,
a boy lost his father
before he could see him smile

a clean demeanor facing the morning sun
where all you may want to read
about how I ended up catching sight
of a moribund countenance
shall appear.

10

A Warning without Warning

In a few hundred yards
I hope to reach my doorstep,
but first must find my way through the darkness

the moon obscured,
lights
in the neighborhood extinguished by the storm,
a tree over the road blocking the narrow bridge.

I'll have to find another way around,
through the area where the criminals live
and the streets
are littered
with broken bottles and cigarette ends

every step preceded by one equally as silent.

What use a heavenly guide?

If it cared it would illumine my path

10: A WARNING WITHOUT WARNING

an aura of invincibility,
at least an insight into the mind of an assailant.

What use the Yi when I can't see the coins
and the way they fall?

Would a reading protect me
from the beating on my skull
or the rush of blood?

What use supplication?

How could my invocation influence the higher powers
to concentrate attention
on my journey
at the expense of maintaining the flow
and fluctuations
of the universe?

I'll creep by, careful to hide my presence

not make a sound,
circumspect as a cat stalking its prey

blend into the night

a chill working through the ends of my fingers,
the suck of fluid through an open ventricle.

10: A WARNING WITHOUT WARNING

Could, though, dismissal forebode ill,
the sense to feel an influence disappear
if I succumb
to the black hollow tapering toward my feet?

One step at a time

yes, but where I put my foot
isn't dependent on clever judgement

I hear a match strike
and place it to the left,
catch a glimpse of an eye
and place it to the right,
an odor of sweat

hold off until it passes

somewhere within, without:

"Watch your step"

rest for a while against a wall.

A few yards more
and I'll be at the lower bridge.

Needless to say, I am relieved

the glow on the other side suspends familiar angles
and curves in a flux brought to a standstill,
the trail behind loathe to penetrate its vicissitudes

the pond where children gather
to collect tadpoles and keep them in glass bowls,
the gate you can lean on
and count butterflies landing on dead leaves.

Haven't there been other times,
in the warmth of satisfaction
or the moist calm preceding an accolade,
I'd be roused from slumber:

"Wake up"

momentum toward a new day saturated with one thought:

I am a solitary wayfarer with no one, it seems,
to take care of a racing heart

even though one I deny
is there in the background taking steps
on the same path beneath a canopy of starless night,
accompanying the while I am on my own.

11
Not Far to Go

Winter
when I was a child
that didn't seem lighter,
fresher and icier
than it does now

it seems colder than I can bear

the feeling in my bones.

Frost reflected morning light,
the twitter of a bird
and the crunch of footsteps to the old school room
anticipated warmth, firelight
and a glance from the girl
who wore a ribbon tied in a strange knot

this morning a trudge to the abandoned shrine
to pray for release from the suffering.

I'll stand my staff against the doorway,
assume a position only the love

for inconsequential facts could emulate
and cross my hands.

The crack disappearing into the floor:

broken skin between my fingers

the web suspended between the sill
and the wall:

shadows
in my eyes

red paint peeling off the lump
of wood in the corner:

the graze upon my lungs

a nest clumped under the eaves:

the effort that sticks clouds and mud together
to suit one's mood

an odor
of early blossom:

11: NOT FAR TO GO

the excuse I gave
to free me from the day's travail
in an orchard,
so I could visit a travelling troupe of circus performers,
"I have lost my cat
and must find her"

the chime of a clock tower:

the walk homewards

a tree sprinkled with snow:

a mother who tried to instill a sense
of the right thing to do

the blue sky:

absence of concern
I would have lived a better life than this moment

the iron gate through which one or two enters
to keep an appointment with a man of means:

the notion,
if I'd have wanted to,
if I had the resources at my disposal
and clear skin, I could have built a bridge
between poverty and accomplishment

over twisting words into patterns no one will read
than the undertaker at the end
or maybe, if the flow is in the right direction,
a traveler from a lonely isle
who likes to run
with the tide and capture things
as they wash up on the beach

a bright pool
of water:

far back as the inception
of a tongue that forbade a progenitor
to assail the past
and iterate the first utterance
that would heal every ailment,
a message from its own time:

"Clear as the bottom sprouting plants
you'll grow to the surface"

the rhythm
of the sea:

the tenderness as you brushed soot
from my white robe, when evening stretched
as far as the planets converging in a dot
you'd call, "an impulse born in heaven",
flicking it off
before stepping into the neighbor's garden
to steal an apple

11: NOT FAR TO GO

returning with sweet,
white acid forming a ring around your lips,
pretending you'd exist equally
as securely in ink filling the bristles
of my brush,
transferring it to my forehead

an old man leaving footprints:

the journey when weight no longer tugs at one's ankles,
air can be breathed easily
and the will
to reinterpret isolated incidents
in a manner said to be one's own
put to rest.

12

Stagnation

A one-eyed man with a spade
in his hand

earth broken into clumps,
roots
and a body contorted in the hole

who deserves no more
than a moment's silence and a few words:

as far as dead eyes can make out—

a bulbous ghost swilling spittle,
blue toads weeping blood

the hack
that wipes away a door,
a leaden wander
on grey bricks

looking at yourself
for a long time

over and again.

Break open that bottle
and pour it down your throat

a slap on the cheek for the budding minstrel
who forgot the next note, a kick
in the shin for a schoolgirl who forgot to say thank you
when handed butter
on her plate for lunch,
a lashing for a child
who cried
because he cried for his mother who cried

tears when you didn't seem interested
in the journey your youngest took
on her way to the mountains last summer,
the expectation that somehow,
sometime or other, you'd close your folder,
put down your pen and coax the little ones to sleep

the wasteland where the family used to go,
dig little holes, put insects in and cover them:

"A lesson in life," you'd say.

However, neglect and tendency to violence
didn't hurt as much as when the door opened
and you weren't standing there

12: STAGNATION

the moon's rays penetrating to your razor on the sink . . .
and it hadn't been used for months:

"Poetic license, off on a journey.
Self-discovery," so you said.

"On the Outer Ring of Saturn

Red rose
melting through a slit,
the scent of woodlice clogging passages
between snow backed hills
and empty drains, a doe crawling
to an eviscerated fawn,
the mouth of a pig
twisted back in a grimace:

peel me a rotten apple,
cake me over with dust
and counter my weight
falling to the floor
with a mixture of lupin scent,
heartbeats made sticky and dreams
of ancient lovemaking."

Nightfall,
the plaintive note sustained through winter:

"Do you really want to leave us?"

12: STAGNATION

Your magnanimous response:

"I'll plunder the temptress's tears
and bring back essence clearer than lacrimation:"

"On the Tender Edge of Rebirth

Splatter time come back to haunt me,
grey magnet pulling me along
like an outer planet."

"From subterranean passages I caressed,
the dictation of one who burns like a star:"

"I'm There Already

Late night involution
on the surf pounding frozen air, breakneck speed
happy to arrive,
all the others in a row to be counted—
wet, dry, blue, green

a little one, a monster and a rainbow in between

cauterize the planets wound
boiling in confusion,
all *they* have to see is one another's rear end,
unfurling space
and the longevity of my intrusion."

12: STAGNATION

Solemn last words for a wretch
who expected greater return
for stenciling his name
on a goddess's inner eye:

where you entered
so will I
if only for the trace she'll leave
with my name written on it,
what you drank so will I
if only
to numb the mood of the poison
that made you splutter and cough
and bring forth images only a fool could engender

in the manner you pronounced, "higher calling,"
so will I
if only the refusal
to repeat a second time
what you produced.

13

A Family of Friends

She couldn't afford a brush
so tied together chewed-on-the-end sticks,
used spittle
and ash to replenish ink
and old rag found in the dump for paper

when dry,
handing her completed work to a small gathering
which appreciates her style
and has little regard
for the means of production

late at night, drinking wine
when the crickets chirp
and the moon rises over the hills,
entering into communion
with the force in her vision:

lineaments born in such depth
they intimate the presence of a musician
whose melodies,
note by note,
reflect a conglomeration
of syllables
the poet embraces when,

13: A FAMILY OF FRIENDS

coursing the winds
of Venus or tasting salt in the depths,
he softens free fall
and its effect upon the heart,
as the scholar finds
when twisting the meaning of an ancient text
to meet readers demands for clarity.

"His hand looks as if it could bend back
with a bamboo stalk in a high wind.

Yes, like the grove behind my study,
flexible
as the presence of a mother to her children
when supper time draws near.

Or,
a barbarian's makeshift instrument,
announcing the candid journey
has ended.

Stroked in expectation
of wide-open legs,
fingerprints on the back
and calm seconds when the waves subside.

His left leg,
suspended
in a goddess's ardor poising above a dandelion
reluctant to crush it.

In the manner, perhaps, of one
who feels the weight of decision,
whether to go forward
or wait until circumstances are propitious,
who could freely ascend to the stars
or retreat to the back room
and pore over a text
for the rest of his life.

And find how moist the buds are,
tender the tips.

Easy to crush life
and leave the remnants to secrete vital juices.

Every petal,
with a gentle twist from actual bearing,
pointing to elements that at any moment,
too, could expect to be bruised
by the fall of an oversized intruder
or broken by the carelessness of idleness.

A spider's web hanging from blades of grass,
an ear hiding from an abundance of commotion.

Yet, with a delicate touch
and dabs hardly touching the surface,
features capturing the love of one
who would expunge suffering from the universe.

13: A FAMILY OF FRIENDS

Scent that fills the wind,
frost
and words chalked upon membrane
stretched between his ears:

"Like a butterfly,
lift your right foot."

The freckle on one eyelid suggesting a family trait
passed down through the ages,
which knew of the flight
into the heavens,
but brought to ground
by misdemeanor.

Deep,
dark eyes.

A creature illuminated by its own inner light,
waves reaching the bottom.

Garb ragged as our own,
feet bare of leather, demeanor
really not so much different
from us all.

Shall we adopt a pose and dance like our friend
who,
though only born out of fantasy,
divulges an identity
in which we can share:

for you to find the plaintive chord,
our bookworm
to draw out in discussion of human nature
and me to turn into a line

quick
as the breath when we stumble,
long as the intake
of late-night aroma

short
as the step
which precedes our bumping into one another?"

14

From out of a Stranger's Heart

While rummaging in the back of the cupboard for something to eat
I found some yellowing pages
discarded most probably decades ago

a previous owner
or his friend who visited
and left things behind,
a young man who put them aside
and forgot them?

A few passages which haven't been obscured by mold.

One step would reach a rock in the stream,
another an ibis waiting for a mate
to signal delight in its presence, a few more
the bank underneath trees shaded by leaves
which have never felt the full glow of an afternoon sun.
Two, three and a hand
will touch structure spanning two edges
brought together for ease of entry
to the next stage of a lifelong walk:

14: FROM OUT OF A STRANGER'S HEART

an abode with a loved one fast
as a pinecone tossed into a furnace,
the plans for a new residence
sketched where a rainbow reaches a raincloud,
the certainty standing before an object
when attention is focused on something more fragile:

the feather on a nest,
a buttercup in a vase,
a paper doll in a child's hand.

I will never be capable of creating the squeezed in the hands and caressed. Alongside whom will I find a piece of night-time that'll keep? Saigyo, Tu Mu or the mad poet who stood under the river that flows from one end of the sky to the other, waiting until the lapping waves carried toward him lines preceding his own journey to seek what could be sustained through time?

I could unravel layers populated by star entranced wanderers, fertilized eggs bleeding into the ocean, a pauper who'd chance his arm against a goddess's in defiance of retribution

far and away.

Shadows
are falling, light
is dimming and I drift
from what I could have been

a hero leading an army,
willing to erect castles

14: FROM OUT OF A STRANGER'S HEART

victory, honor,
mine

an emperor's right hand stalking the thrones of snake people,
fossicking amongst ruins
for gems of amber and turquoise

sweetheart to the mistress
who thanked me
for one illicit night

who'd stay infidel dreams spilling under the gates,
suffocating the guardian,
darkening the temple

evening clouds building over my skull.

The columns holding me are melting
into the soft silence of the earth
and I follow ineluctably into her heartbeat
meeting my dispersion ...

nowhere ...

and faintly behind me

a lover
who never brushed her cheek,

14: FROM OUT OF A STRANGER'S HEART

a vagabond who couldn't climb the ridge,
a warrior who never fought.

Dreams may come and surface to be shared, but, still, even in their most terse and alluring passages through the night will never be sensed like snow in the eyes or water cascading from above douching the figure beneath and numbing it into somnambulance:

At intervals of minutes,
another blossom will come alive to the open air,
another bud swell
in anticipation of becoming a flower,
another mind address the interior with the same intensity
as a million insects swarming to the focus of enjoyment
and, at the same time,
when snow has receded from the peaks,
the wind has lost its coldest edge,
another creaturely mortal sense the mid-morning sun
and open to its surroundings
where death is never felt in vain.

With no expectation, or thought it may ever happen, from out of the last millennium or the future looking back on the second that preceded last night and the planets converging above the hearts that knew one another before the sun nourished the first animal that crept, looking for its first meal, the strange inkling that she isn't another whim caught sighing in the treetops:

the boil on my cheek,
sunset,
late as usual

14: FROM OUT OF A STRANGER'S HEART

a spare seat, a patch over an eye,
a longer glance than I would
if I were crossing the street

a second that meant more
than the whole evening's entertainment,
lemon juice set aside
for later, a bud on the table.

"So, you collect tea leaves as well.

I have a few from China."

"I won't go on about myself.
I'll only accompany you
if you see fit."

What a gorgeous sprinkle of light in your hair

our daughter's voice
the sound of rain
so youthful.

Alongside my own I'll store them,
making sure that every page
will be available to be read tomorrow
and in a few years' time

as long as fire doesn't curl toward the center,
an unseasonal thunderstorm doesn't wash them down the drain
and the new owner keeps them as a memento
of years gone by.

15
Humility

Wanting to spread its wings
in a lamp on the sideboard,
but diminishing the presence
of self
to a translucent end,
a moth descends toward my toe
and settles.

Is it tired,
lonely, injured?

Does an obstruction prevent it
from following its normal course
or the echo of a time when its legs stuck in honey

(but was picked up and released)

return to reawaken its vow
to never desert a friend?

Appreciating its consideration, but acknowledging
it would grow fearful in the lower depths,

15: HUMILITY

I shake my foot and allow it to make its way
where it can best unfold natural inclination.

Ascending with care
not to overreach an approach
that can be breathed in,
it'll allow powder to mingle with warmth
and the blaze immolate the opposite supposing the earth hard
and solid.

Emptying the capacity
to calculate why the moon is full,
the road long yet less travelled
and the miles in front clear,
I shall cross the falling down bridge
without stopping in the middle, listen
for the wind through the leaves

yet,
configured in bones that still feel the weight
of marrow seeping into the calves,
kick the dust

every pebble reminding me
of the face
I met in childhood:

a relative moving a tear
shed a thousand miles away,
who suffered a fall
simply walking alongside the river

edges giving way under her feet,
bruising scarlet flowers
and sinking.

Recounting the times when she gave time
to clean old sores
and bind them with rags,
I'll call down the brilliant moon
and caress her into life

turn the heartache into a flame,
acid into water
and the bruise on her spines into a sheen

in expectation of touching dead limbs
with the color in my dreams,
suppose she could lift from her place of finality
and resume her walk.

Asking for one last descent
near to the body that brightens moonlight
and the unaccompanied
that fly from frozen wastelands,
she reminds me that I dwell below the cares
that drift into a web of listening
and she above the dust
where they may be answered:

"Leave the fruit of evolving millennia
to an immortal clothed in white,
take up your cudgel

15: HUMILITY

and beat the ground once before you take a step
and once again before you take another

for the sound,
in the moment it arises,
cancels the other sounds
that impel a moist, but blurred eye
into believing it can see rays from blue incendiaries:

"You can be
whatever you want to be"

foam on an incoming wave
into an elixir fresh as a raindrop:

"There is nothing
that you can't do"

an underfed sleepwalker
who aims to listen to boughs breaking in nocturnal storms
into a thrice gilded orator
who can cajole widows into parting with loneliness,
bear witness to hierarchies
which reach unlived in rose beds
and denote the times a transparent body floats above a bone
that simply needs bracing in a splint:

"All the world is an oyster
and you
are the pearl.""

16
A Kindred Spirit

Over the water—

a note
from a stringed instrument, a thump
on a drum

one
after the other, becoming louder,
until the valley resonates with song evoking the deeds
of an adventurer
who, in step with each beat,
accepted long odds
in a quest
to find mountains where the gods reside

into the clouds

curved sword and staff
as companion.

Faced with an avalanche
he sheltered under an outcrop,
meeting the iciest winds

16: A KINDRED SPIRIT

knelt behind a tree, tormented
with thought of never arriving
drank a potion left by a soothsayer

successor to a kingdom
where day burns the early hours

clear headed,
through gilded snow, ascending the peak

a nest
egg-robbers can never espy

a vein in his brain channeling beyond the sun,
head bent toward receding light.

Many
will savor rhythms nearing the threshold,
sit for hours listening to breath fade
on the ridge:

"We never knew
you would leave, couldn't think about it—

an eggshell breakfast
with mustard"

a few,
who'll make out the place

where they've always lived,
cross where light lands on their hearts

kittens on the back steps,
a signpost pointing out the way to the next town,
a healer
who looks after sore feet:

"We'll plunge into the marketplace,
help a stranger find her way,
assist a child ties his lace
and,
when the band is in tune,
sing of a mortal who reached the goal"

another,
who couldn't reach the foothills,
bring to mind a predecessor
who glanced sideways
at the sun
and bade night creatures share his dreams

through blood stained eyes—

the whitest face:

"I found no solace
in your friendship,
little to gain
from wavering between two worlds—

16: A KINDRED SPIRIT

a ghost sheltering in rain swept corridors

moisten dead lips
to hear
of frost-bitten hands lifting a sword,
cruelty
in shivering glands—

a spleen leaking what little light it had
to sustain it

seek you in fear
the days will curdle,
rainbows go green,
the heart drench with phoenix tears

because I love you.

Dedicated to Li He (790–816)

17
Inner Light

Under smog the city below refuses to quieten:

a neural wail,
chug of a train taking coal
to the hinterland

an ungracious reply
to another broken heart,
a pulse stained with blood outside the vein.

I'll drink from the stream
you'd have crossed,
pluck twigs
that hint of age-old forests
about to reveal their essence
to a stranger:

mold,
earth smelling clumps
that unfurl emerald green

rotten pith,
sun warmed edges

the pungent muck
that sticks a finger to a thumb,
an obscure poet
who carried a satchel containing brush
and ink, simple fare
like a Buddhist monk

the present
in a transparent shrine:

a rock,
a shoot under a foot,
blue veins around the ankles

little man
of no name, snow will cover you
and you will light the fire inside.

A welcoming sign
on the inn:

"Here you can enjoy a meal, a bath,
a drop of liquor

when the shutters close
nothing will disturb you
except,
maybe, an ember failing to ignite,
snowflakes on the roof,
a gentle wakeup call:

17: INNER LIGHT

In the morning
continue on your way."

The road
is leading where your heart would

free
to wander

the glow
on the trees,
night smeared under the leaves

in accord with the overarching goal
to step in the footsteps
of one who'll only let on
that he loves you
when shadows cross your eyes,
tinctures of blue color your breath
or the pain brings you to your knees

who some will give a name,
many their obedience
and,
enduring the tear
at the fabric keeping the heart inside,
barely able to see the master's footprints,
follow

temperature dropping below freezing.

17: INNER LIGHT

Sounds of industry reach the hills
and, with the intent to form mounds
and depressions, charged particles
and substance bearing the weight of unlimited need,
fracture listening

or,
the aftermath of summer's retreat brings silence
fine
as light, full as the sea,
to settle around the ears.

"There are windows to be cleaned,
irregular verse
to be composed
and, if you are in a good mood,
old men and old ladies
to be cheered up
by visiting them in the hostel."

18

Renewal

I leave dirty utensils overnight,
neglect the garden overgrown with weeds

mold covers the ceiling.

Injuries inflicted on a child
hold no interest

I couldn't care whether it lives
or dies
as long as I don't have to hear its needy cries
or the father berating its stupidity.

Literature stored under the sink resonates with poverty

unaccustomed to light,
devoid of vitality,
the imperative to contemplate teeming depths
forsworn in a miasma of week-old egg white
and wine fumes

it should be scattered across the room
and stamped on.

Lay down
in tall reeds,
smell the acrid mud

the tiniest cell ceasing to call
for the will
to be elsewhere,
pebbles covered one
by one

allow my heart to run
on the ripples,
a bubble bursting on the surface,
an insect's shrill voice?

So long ago, hardly seen,
it could have been the arrival
of a new baby
who took all the attention of mother
while you lay in your own dirty rags,
or the beatings endured
at the hands
of an enraged father.

Further back,
an imperial guard who fled the services
of his Lord

18: RENEWAL

in the one night of curdling veins,
seduced a favorite
and left her lying outside the brightly lit courtyard

stones built up to mark the space
where he lay down in his own fluid,
sleet that covers the stain
before the ice melts,
a blade hardened in the extreme

likeness to those who never knew why either.

Confer with anyone who could look into five places
at the same time?

The old girl who charges one coin
for a consultation

draws blood from a sore limb,
lets it drip
and splash open like a flower

wraps a broken bone in warm hands,
allows the moisture penetrate the discolored stuff
until it meets the fresh part beneath

draws out your innards and deposits them
where the moon lights up their tenderness?

18: RENEWAL

So far back,
when even sentient creatures
couldn't fathom the depth of their own shallowness,
before the mortal remains
of an immortal descent
and the uncomfortable moans from an earthbound dwelling,
the wistful ardor that one could,
if today was entwined with tomorrow
and yesterday aligned
with now,
stay forever in the tepid drifting by
and never submerge
where paths are cleaned by incoming squalls,
another heart can be said to be alive
and luminous in need
to be prolonged into hearing the other's heart

still,
however,
as air transfuses into blood,
ether
into marrow,
feel the weight of a teardrop,
the delicacy in a powdered wing
or the end
before winter strips the trees bare,
ice closes over the running river
and the call that could renew unearthly parts
issues out of nowhere:

moistened lips speaking of drought,
tensile partitions blocking out harmful rays,
uncultivated fields bringing forth clusters
of chrysanthemums and dandelion.

18: RENEWAL

Windowpanes rattle,
a draught enters a crack
in the floorboards and circles a spider's web

I shall clean every surface, dig out the weeds.

Beams illuminate the hole I'm meant to patch

tomorrow, I promise,
I'll take a present to the mother

chocolate wrapped in a leaf.

An eye bulges in its socket,
lights up underwater green,
watches legs emerge
from limpid skin

I'll kick away from the mud,
surface on an old pond

claim a stalk
where my toes hold fast.

19

Something You'll Leave Behind

At the crossroads before the weather turns sour
choose the least muddy,
expect rain will make each equally forbidding

watch the ducks swim in search of a quiet resting place,
but cross
where traffic passes by in a hurry

get to the mouth of the river
where sunlight glints on the waves,
traverse the rapids
where white water splashes
and drenches the skin

creep through an area where thieves linger
and prostitutes attract the worst clientele,
make it to your house propped against the hill

spend a while clearing weeds
that prevented access to your pond

a bubble spiraling unexplored realms,
crossing a stretch

19: SOMETHING YOU'LL LEAVE BEHIND

of blue,
bursting on the surface

at the day's end,
with no hesitation, knock at your door

eyes reading the color of my mood,
sunset reddening the furrows in a brow,
lips greeting me with kindness:

"I have waited
a while, almost thought
you wouldn't make it

what say we look
at the one discarded by your old friend
destined never to be read

(almost)

and laugh:

knapsack full of wild herbs,
wayfarer bound for tomorrow's yesterday

springtime in his gait"

one log following another into the fire,
a dry countenance growing greyer by the hour.

19: SOMETHING YOU'LL LEAVE BEHIND

I can only guess
at the springs of meditation
as you didn't last until the summer.

The night I made my way back across the river,
realizing it'd be me who'd return
to light the candles surrounding your death bed,
you hoped to leave a few words,
if she were still alive, I could pass on
to a mother whom you left without saying goodbye:

"I looked to you for comfort
in my hour of need,
transforming worry into silence
and absence of sustenance into plenty.

With your forethought nurturing my every step,
I rose from the cradle,
aware that I,
who longed for companionship
to offset grasping for light
in solitude,
would never develop into a self-respectful human
without your loving devotion.

So,
I hugged you with tenderness,
stroked your chin with an outstretched finger
and playfully twined your hair.

With no reserve
of sentiment crying for the torrid winds

19: SOMETHING YOU'LL LEAVE BEHIND

to abate on a moist brow,
called you,
"My Dearest.""

Dust settles on a coffin,
the smell of scented water reaches tired nostrils
and passing feet disappear into the night

mention, absentmindedly,
to the one and only relative,
how the icy finger will select each
and every one
of us one day

a slow path made out to escape the clamor,
an aura around the body
that will take months to disappear

a heart throbbing like a nightingale's
redolent with heat of a companion,
the emptiness under your feet channeling the same whispers
as the space behind your eyes:

"I'll edge toward the windblown reed,
the frond cascading to my forehead

a teardrop hanging from my lash

swallow two droplets
of nectar

lose contact with the purposeful realm
outside the bristles of my paintbrush,
unsure of distinguishing wooden limbs
from bony hands,
petals from unblemished skin,
pebbles
from fingernails

stars from sleep."

Mercury rises,
the morning star seems a little brighter

notice the yellow
in an eye and the blotch on a forehead

in the gilt-edged mirror my friend delighted in,
two or three handing around the little book
in which he kept the verses
and phrases skirting the edge of Martian plains
or burrowing into a mushroom under moonlight:

"Scrape the surface
to ensure enough is gathered
to tell what constitutes our nearest neighbor,
place instruments in the path
of emanations from the sun,
sip clear fluid
that doesn't flow
in runnels crisscrossing the dust

make believe you have entered rarefied air
that could,
if escaping from lungs that spread from inertia
to molten rock,
sustain a life form
far nobler than the multitude left behind.

We have ventured further than ever before,
placed our feet on untrodden soil,
seen from a distance our own land appear on the horizon,
our own verdant land, blue and white
in space black as a nightmare."

Embedded in gristle
a tearful eye passes over the smudges
where a soothsayer invited a resolute warrior into his heart:

"One pattern of the sixty-four
in shadow or in light dazzling on the stone
upon which I rest my head
will disclose whether gloom will ensue
or the lark sing,
whether it is opportune
to advance to a goal suppressing a marauder
or wait
until the wind has died
and all is still
before contemplating movement . . .

the mandate of Heaven . . .

19: SOMETHING YOU'LL LEAVE BEHIND

and I, incarcerated by a tyrant,
will,
in accordance
with the meanings becoming clearer
from manipulation
of the stalks found here and there
embedded in layers of dust,
surely, as a heron crossing the wide river
that flows between higher ground
and the sea,
rise from captivity and strike him down."

With dawn springing into new life,
having held your unsteady hand,
an egret struggles
to crack the final layer encasing its wings,
a solitary cloud dies in the mist

at a point
where a flake of ash enters the same point
where what I expect
in a gentle wave
will appear on the horizon.

20

From Different Points of View

Instead of pushing forward without respite,
why not rest for a while
and shine a lamp on the drift rising above your head?

Does it remind you of a life without birdsong,
the chorus contained in a worldly theatre,
bury the green and red
she picks to brighten her room,
reflect the white
of her eye where tears well
when the one she loves
has bidden goodbye?

Or, finding a dry nook,
listen to the snow pounding against stone?

What will happen
when blood drains from each socket
and ash
is drenched with rain?

Will the observer forever remain alone,
in lieu
of cheek to cheek contact,

infuse the night
as another shadow slides into a backdrop
for a star
to appear

(an immense conflagration)

unimpeded
by lemon stinging a cut between eyelid and eyesight,
swing toward a plane
that will never be felt,
sworn to live or be anything other
than which is not there?

Will the rising moon adopt a new face
devoid of blemish,
distil the gleam in a conqueror's eye,
keep clear in the firmament
inanimate to those only
whose light proceeds from dying centers
no one will visit

endlessness so near
it could have happened before it started,
distance so close
the echo abounds in the word
before it occurred?

I don't particularly want empty weightlessness
nor do I prefer to face the time of the end
or an assurance I may be sustained
in the luxury of love.

20: FROM DIFFERENT POINTS OF VIEW

Couldn't I simply concentrate
on how close I could come
to the edge
without falling over?

"I have no qualms about your intransigence,
but is it possible
to disabuse you
of the singular need for aspiration:

you must separate from the throng,
drugged on abstinence
and fulfilled with severity,
litter the transcendent path with excuses
how you can't face daily travail

the moment
of light bursting through the veil of denial
imminent."

"Autumnal squalls warm as puppy's breath,
winter storm
quiet as a ray of sunshine

a catchment for ingress
of flight without boundaries,
a touch strewn with kindness

taste of sweat
like liquid sugar,
dishwater resonating morning dew

coarse grit choking each pore,
letting through the finest threads discoverable
on ethereal apparel

bones pressing into soil,
smoothing wrinkles deep as an ancient well

a newborn lathed in oil
as it screams an arrival?"

"I cannot see
but sense lunar power enveloping my frame,
cannot hear but tune to the depths apportioning a probability
I could have occurred elsewhere but didn't,
cannot articulate why liquid trickles into an indentation,
the second
between one flake brushing a nape
and another falling into space
no other will explore seems like an eternity
but whisper:

I feel drawn to ascend
when I follow the rhythms that breathe
to the full extent an opposite will allow,
disappear
when heat is at its most intense,
return to a keener feeling
of my own self boundary
when crunching beneath the footsteps
of a black clad figure
ice has encrusted the road."

20: FROM DIFFERENT POINTS OF VIEW

"All night long I have waited
till I was strong enough to reveal a pattern
in the furrows crisscrossing hedges, frozen streams
and wooden gates unable to open.
Beneath me a figure trudges toward his home.
What could he hope to achieve?

The drag suggests fatigue,
a bowed head the refusal to turn back,
closed eyes resisting a memory which rested
in the arms of a lover,
now so far away,
still hoping she will see him again."

"Even if I meant to penetrate every open shaft,
eventually I would meet blazing fire
and melt
till every memory of my stark overcoat dissipates

yet,
now,
the heart's intent to reach the end of the road
is mine
to destroy
if only I can find the veins leading to the center:

the groan of an ancient waterwheel coming to a halt,
fingers caught in the revolution,
no one about to render assistance

the black glow."

20: FROM DIFFERENT POINTS OF VIEW

"Will he plant the trinket I gave him gave him
in the drift

the dalliance meant nothing to him,
everything to me

grit his teeth against the cold

cheerless sojourns preferable to delight
which means thinking about someone else
more than himself?"

21

I'll Get to You Somehow

Couldn't I disregard
how you undermined my confidence
by scattering reams
of paper on the lake?

My appeal:

violets are blue like heaven's descent

my sacred offering:

rain sprinkled iris,
planets converging in the black center,
no distance between us

words you'll treasure:

"How much
I feel for you at night"

black rivulets seeping to the bottom:

21: I'll Get to You Somehow

"Find another."

I'll carve our initials until the sap fills the grooves

(you would only cut down the tree)

join cobwebs in the rafters and catch the fly

(and then what . . . eat it?)

borrow a love potion from an enchantress
and sprinkle it on your food

(you'd find the antidote of fresh, clean water).

I'll crawl behind the headstone,
push all the pencil ends
that have gathered over the past month
into a heap
and pen another sincere appeal
to a heart I hope will respond favorably:

In land rarely visited,
I'll find a thread linking the deep hollow
to a cloudburst,
gently pick off the end
and transfer it into my fingers,
unsteady, at best,
tune it

21: I'll get to you somehow

to the highest vibrations between Andromeda and Orion,
so the occupant will never be submerged

(I truly feel
for the plight of all creatures)

entertain the favor
of gods wrestling with lower incumbents,
affix our names
to the eternal threshold

(I know you like to keep things simple)

plant a seed

it will grow profusely

you'll be wide eyed with wonder
at how quickly it will spread and cover a trellis,
blocking the sun's harmful rays

(I know how delicate your skin is).

Your heart stained with grief
will linger no more on the border
between livid watchfulness
and the morbid vow threatening to cross

(a head you'd cradle in your arms)

the black gate swung open to catch the air
gelid from his lips
stay bolted,
my longing framed in ancient script
and tomorrow's reinterpretation:

In any age there is so much to live for

(I am truly convinced we would hone
each other's sharpest weapons).

The moon will shine through rain
and lighten up midnight

it will at that

(and that it will again)

a spot of blood
on the back of a hand,
a glistening thorn

a solitary widow always go
where her husband was buried

21: I'll get to you somehow

an ear numbed with cold,
pink insides

and I will pour out my heart

even though it'll escape your interest,
have no value in monetary terms,
no relevance
to the world
at large

because your force to survive
still haunts my backbone.

22

Beauty

The scrawl upon white paper,
a drop
of ink,
afternoon glow brightening each sentence

the close
to the heart hope
I'll renew the impetus
to discover what lies under my skin,
the scrape
of a fingernail, ancient names

empty shadow,
uninhabited glade,
Saturday's work crunched up
and thrown in a receptacle

the notepad used to collect random observations,
a dirty teacup, dishes covered with yesterday's meal

a crack in my back as I stand up,
the splashes,
rattles
and crashing about as I clear up the mess,
absence of activity as I put them away until tomorrow

22: BEAUTY

an old book I've held on to since boyhood,
yellowing pages,
must in my nostrils, the rustle
when I examine the next picture I know so well:

a swallow's curve against the pale blue sky,
light behind the trees,
a young man
with a knapsack

a splinter working into a toe,
sap rising with orange blisters,
a mouse fleeing to a leaf strewn stump

a creak in dead limbs as the wind rises from the east,
clouds beyond tinged with black,
the first few drops upon the canopy overhead

an old trunk still alive
despite the waterline up to its lower branches,
a shoreline surrendering to breakers willing themselves to the cliffs,
foam,
debris and red flowers left on the tideline

the pristine call
of a warbler,
the response from another in the woods,
silence as they find one another

every second belonging to a ripple on a lake,
haze in the distance,

22: BEAUTY

the fall
and rise of lonely breath

the luminous bird fluttering over the waves before sleep.

23

Netherworld

I found out that the old woman
who sold pink carnations under lamplight
was accosted, her meagre takings stolen
and the pendant
she wore around her throat torn away.

Where could the assailant hide?

Under the floorboards
of the toilet
in the school grounds, between the skirts
of his lover,
in the gutted playhouse
where no one bothers to recite words
that once excited the crowd
and raised their temperature
in spite of the cold outside?

Where he deigns to breathe
I'll strike a light
and illumine his hare lip,
prize open his eyelid and extract the fluid
that enabled him to perceive what didn't belong to him

with the memory of the woman's bruise
I'll leave the same mark
where he likes to sing to his children

(they adopt the same broken palate
as he).

While the circle continues to contract around his fear
I'll call on the agency of lustrous being
to disclose his whereabouts, each step
will bear the weight
of the past that carries every foul deed
he enacted
before he met his latest victim
whose back faced his front.

While the search
in the immediate vicinity seeks to locate the criminal
in his dark place
he'll take a flower taken from the lady's tray
and recite lugubriously
as each petal is torn from the stem:

"They won't
find me . . .

they'll find me . . .

they won't find me."

Inspired with dreams of unborn kittens,
secure with thoughts of a blind dog chasing stars
and satisfied with a broken fingernail, spittle
and the back of a hand
he'll draw a capital I,
follow it with an M, raise his strength
to complete the POT,
remind himself he knows how to spell ENT
and watch it drip
to his fingers.

Awake
to the drumming in my temple,
ready to cross wires with a luminous beast
and replete
with the turning wheel bruising kidneys

hack off what he has written.

24

Rejuvenation

Thinking of my friend
I haven't seen
for a year:

"Don't allow the wind in

it will blow out the candle."

"We need fresh air."

"Excuse me
for not giving my room a sweep
or scraping mold off the floorboards

it is all
I can do to scribble in my notebook."

"Never mind,
wipe a patch where I can sit under the window."

24: REJUVENATION

"Don't say there is more to life
than a bubbling pot on a stove,
the fire underneath
and the stew eaten
while the ashes cool

every fiber
in our bodies
must be provided for."

"At first light, gaze
in awe at the night sky,
count the stars
and raise your light
and love
into the dark expanse

when you've had your fill,
the spring washing blood and water into your marrow
will bring up questions beyond the clatter
of empty plates."

"There's no need
to convince me
dreams drift above nocturnal sojourns

a grey chill forms the outer limit."

"Although the moon
can be seen as one, sharp line,
the hidden center spreads fear
on dark rays

a drop in temperature
when the surface bubbles."

"Suppress the urge to shine light on my tears

they are meant to spring up for no reason."

"How will you soothe them

by blaming a wanton few for your ills,
the fool next door for the rent
in sobriety
and blind chance for the scar on your forehead?"

Calling on my friend who found accommodation
in the dilapidated monastery
converted into a men's shelter:

"The other night, rediscovering what you said,
for want
of a sympathetic ear,
would be from a moment
when I could return to distant climes,
reappear in my own rickety bed,
flavor milk drink with rose,
I wrote it down in my old notebook:"

Wipe dust clinging to the window,
allow the glow

24: REJUVENATION

to reach the ancestral urn upon the mantel,
divulge another secret, at least,
from the heart mingling snow
and ash
and dry your eyes

an invalid who decomposed when you turned the sod
will seek only your semblance,
a neglected child
cut short before her time
will reach only
as far as your wake

the afflicted who'd drown you in unpalatable fluid
congeal in one exclamation:

"I forgive you."

Caress a dove's wing if you can catch it,
anoint your spine with scented oil
if you can reach it,
squeeze her hand when you release it.

The sky 'll be blue,
grey and wet, the clouds black,
voluminous
and white, the earth rich,
brown and creeping with animal life

every second,
rife with the future seen from a moment

24: REJUVENATION

that will pass,
thankful
for passing.

Bedsprings will creak,
a caretaker rise
to check whether the pipes have thawed

the old bell
which hasn't rung for years
ready to receive its first shake.

25

Conscience

In the fields where ice clings to the moon
a second away from birdsong
I blink an eyelid,
taste the sweat on my upper lip
and clench my fist

on the watch for a flame in the sky

no

endless emptiness,
a head with nothing in it

bones sharp at the end

yes, the dawn brings the oak tree into view,
heaven reaches into the earth when we least expect it

a golden halo surrounds the bole

25: CONSCIENCE

less so, forgoing the wonders of the night,
now that my stupid neighbor
has promised to direct his ire when I am not looking

for,
without warning
I cut off a branch above his hovel and shattered the roof

it was an accident, but he,
in his infinite grasp
on the appropriate manner to act,
has determined to do me no good.

I could have taken flight,
summoned him to an arena
or pretended I never encountered anything
to perturb my peace of mind.

Which way?

Whatever seemed best at the time,
instinctively
and without reserve?

Look him in the eye without fear,
disappear into the rain washing away my tracks
or count the days till the lunar eclipse hid the glow
that could have shown the path?

25: CONSCIENCE

Remember what my father said,
"Always stand your ground, son."
Throw the oracle and follow its injunctions
or obey the inner word:

"It's not time to act—
all will be well?"

So I offered him the sweets
my mother had wrapped for the anniversary of her burial

he refused them on the grounds
that nothing could compensate for the damage,
even if I sent flowers moist with dew
that never felt the ill winds
from the factories in the valley
he would stick them where my mother used to pat.

Yes, I know he's an impulsive fool
always threatening to carry out retaliation,
even though days later he calms down
and accepts offers of help and reconciliation.

But, what if this time . . . ?

I'll wring his bloody neck
if he takes one step near me,
smash the rest of his home with a mallet

that will really give him something
to be vindictive about.

Even if sorrow were to pour from *his* lungs,
I'll remind him of my erstwhile honest intention
to make up for what I had destroyed,
the fact I would have liked nothing better
than to co-exist at a distance,
but with respect for each other's path

even though
I think him an idiot,
we could have drawn water from the well together

but no, it's too late

I'll get him from behind

he won't see my feint, my approach

the unearthly guide
who brings out a resounding "no"
when I am filing pins in his brain
and aiming ill will at his neck.

26

Clear-headedness

On the odd occasion,
I spend an afternoon
in the unkempt burial grounds

straggly plants drop wilted heads
across the mound,
light rain seeps
into cracks between barely opened lids.

Someone else has dropped by
with the intention, perhaps,
of channeling poignant vestiges
that still linger
even though a year has passed
since she touched his forearm.

Did she,
like me, bring a pencil
and easily shredded tissue,
meet the remains that still breathe
in regions where the body can't make prints
and, supposing words have been said
for millennia,
try to recover them:

26: CLEAR-HEADEDNESS

white poppies bloom in the ditch

at night I'll creep out,
crush a few and eat them . . .

the shape of the moon
needs someone to contain it
in the black pool
of an eye

I'll sever it
from its orbit, let it sink
into polished landscapes:

hold still

open the window, allow the air
to circulate . . .

a Lord can't ride
on powdered wings fluttering through fire,
he would rather capture the moon
and encircle it
with compassion

it leads a lonely life
and follows the same course
day in
and day out

26: CLEAR-HEADEDNESS

oh,
how he would liberate it, to fly
out of sight
of the heart that would devour it . . .

hold still

pull down the blind,
keep out dead ball eyes . . .

a Lord is in no mood
for visitors
and will attend to them at daybreak,
in tepid air when dreams have rolled
out of sight
he'll read the text lost to a world
unable to elucidate
between nothingness
and emptiness:

when the earth was populated with luminaries
who could read the stars
and follow their instruction
a lonely solitaire revealed their dying wish:

your body is a temporary abode,
you'll live in the darkness beyond the moon,
the supernal blue night,
and evince the moment before it happens
comfortable
with what you know

26: CLEAR-HEADEDNESS

will come to pass
as you want it:

I'll love the heartbeat
of a child
equally as I'll adore an old man
about to face his last moment:

you could have given me a seat
on the veranda
in earshot of a spider clinging to its web,
but the seat in the garden encounters the flight
of a bee

you could have apportioned an adequate portion
of rice
with a sprinkling of sugar,
but a spoonful of millet
goes down well with water

I could, for all time,
savor green fields
and a small child skipping to the tune
of liberation, but,
unable to make out much more
than a blur beyond my immediate vista

the chatter of friends floating toward the abyss

in time with the old clock,
which always strikes the hour,

26: CLEAR-HEADEDNESS

hours later,
tell if the peach tree that struggles to survive
where they planted it in the shade
is able to resuscitate thoughts lingering under its misshapen bent:

petals:

billowing sails,
a journey to exotic destinations

fruit:

globules of oil,
slipping on moonbeams

the kernel:

my itinerant son
who nestles amongst the pines on cold horizons,
traverses the desert where blue skinned travelers pass,
or,
further from home
when he must pay for his far-flung adventures,
harvesting crops on the fringes of a wilderness

a stranger:

not in the main orchard,
but secreted in a grove where the sun hardly penetrates,

26: CLEAR-HEADEDNESS

I come across clusters
of red berries that glow
even in the shade

rather than pluck them,
I'll leave them
until they drain the earth of moisture,
turn a darker shade
and swell
until bursting

select a few that have fallen by the way,
plant then
where they may be eaten by another wanderer
who'll take them closer
to one
who may savor their strangeness:

a sparrow hops to my feet
and pecks at the seed
I had dropped,
eying me
in the anticipation of another handful

yet,
I have run out

never mind,
the seasons will produce the same
over and again

26: CLEAR-HEADEDNESS

I'll be able to let fly
into the wind more nourishment,
find another handful
on another day

wait

if I can squeeze my hand
into the jar

I can scrape the contents off the bottom:

twisted saplings make a fence
around the grave where my father lies

now bones
and a skull disturbed by roots pushing though the eye socket

someday, I will lie beside him

tangled growth no longer an obstacle
to sharing the acidic daydreams of a woebegone generation
and what will flower
when all the fumes
have blown into the sea.

27

Nourishment

An empty bowl, a child's palm

night before the clink
of coins or the shifting of sticks

noodle soup
and pepper, a cube
of sugar to nibble

luminous accompaniment
and sensitive response
translating into confident movement
or retreat

a spurt of wine into a drunkard's mouth,
healing him
so he can face the demands of loneliness

notes for the musician
to play, a listener to enjoy

the mood preceding an encore,
anticipating the end

rapture,
light—
transient
yet where one has been will always be—
a smile and a nod

fine air, ice
at the fringes,
leaves like swords

an ibis drawn on a vase

a cloudburst
for the parched earth

enough to make the forest luxuriant,
rivers flow,
but too much
for the ants to build another nest.

After the flood has receded
I assist a young farmer find some mementos
of his children
lost a few days before

this is her cup,
this her plaything

27: NOURISHMENT

a shard
of pottery,
a stone painted with lacquer.

I could leave a poem strung together
with tears and shame
but he'd prefer a bud his daughter sought
on the branch

before it began to rain.

28

Overwhelmed

It could be the drain
clogged with peelings, the swig
from a brown bottle,
the cat bringing up fur balls,
a cough raising discharge
onto a mirror

a noisome puddle
under the floorboards,
the bruise on your daughter's cheek,
a stain
on both sides of the kitchen mat,
blubbing I hear too often

hours slipping on a tempo
I can't constrain:

candles to be lit,
the mangy cat
still waiting to be petted
after weeks of inattention,
a midnight visit
to the outhouse to be attended to

28: OVERWHELMED

another scream unignorable.

If I were to breathe where a stone has no outside—

still,
where a cataract flows over the edge—

you would give me the strength
to brings the polarities from the deep
into the heights and nebulas
into a raindrop,
expunge the offending material
and allow the waste
to disperse

face the idiot next door
and assert an authority
that can smell sulphur and taste ash
on the back of the neck

the hand, then
maybe, will fall gently.

A warm gust springing from behind the trees—

an admonishment?

"He would only bite you
with yellow teeth."

28: OVERWHELMED

Tufts of grass
on the hill between the road and the shed
he calls a house bending towards torn curtains—

a moist stick across his back?

"He'll break in and steal every page
you have been working on for a year."

A rusted gate,
a thorn bush sprawled over the path:

"Watch out
for razor sharp twigs."

Corrugated sheets held down with large stones,
doors hanging on
with string,
a crack in the wall
you could put your fist through:

"Do you really have a warriors' claws?"

The flicker that lifts a lid
and lets in sight
of silver wings
and unsullied skin disappearing before they happen:

28: OVERWHELMED

"Can you cross over and steep long-ago ailments
with the light of renewal,
alleviate his ache of having to face his last moments
over and again?"

Even if I lift a finger,
you won't teach me the right moves
at the right time.

I'll stand on my own two feet.

The skull bones cheerless smile taking up the full frame
of the window—

soiled underwear in a corner, splotches
on the floor,
the colander full of bile:

"Must you make so much of a racket
and abuse your children

if you don't desist, I'll call the authorities."

The moon's ray falling on a grey lagoon—

an emperor who'd transfuse your fluid
into his
to make him sound,
call down the clouds to slake his thirst,

28: OVERWHELMED

temper his brow
with the flow between Heaven and Saturn,
bleach every stained membrane
with juice from his daughter's lungs:

"What business is it of yours?"

A tethered lover gliding around in tighter circles
until the rope strangles her:

"Sew up your windpipe."

A somnambulant imbibing froth—

hungry ghosts who cannot accept the end
and can't exceed the moment before the end,
scales
and lips floating to the surface:

"Charnel your cat."

Pursuant to a stiff brush
and fizzing white powder,
liquid gurgling
and a downward rush,
the sweet, clean smell
of fresh water

28: OVERWHELMED

faint as wind chime tone touching naked membrane
stretched between December
and January:

"Don't show your face.
He will still do you harm."

I'll leave the mat
in a tub to soak,
keep a gnarled rod by the fireplace

in the early hours,
when the embers die down and the lamps go out,
without obscuring moonlight seeping through the gaps
and cracks,
make my way to bed

the cat's sores to be looked at
in the morning.

29
Peril

I stumbled over a root
and cut my lip

inanimate as it is
I'll gouge it out
and burn it
as I would any obstacle

the shadow stains fallen limbs,
surrounds
on all sides

the lantern broken
and I can't remember
where I put the candle

the roar of a waterfall

so close
I can imagine each droplet falling,
lost in the pond

29: PERIL

likewise
every corpuscle resonates with the descent

at midnight chasing the stars
because they hurt the expanse of self-absorption
without breathing anew,
the inward momentum
without looking outwards

an impulse
to become all that there can be

bone matter saturated
with tears:

the bench where a woman watches a sparrow peck
at crumbs

"Tickle us
with entrails":

an expletive
from the butcher
when a delinquent told him his sausages
were inedible

a mannequin cackling behind shutters
as I sliced the tendon under her lover's ardor:

29: PERIL

the tailor's wife tracing a pattern

the moonbird's plumage
redder than the cough
out of the old warrior:

fresh paint on the barber's window ledge

refusal to heed a warning:

"It isn't time to take a walk
when you are recovering from an illness."

30

Lost in Light

I'll carry my pen
and ink on this trip with the intention
to jot down the most insignificant of things:

back lanes radiating from the central square,
an enclosed temple,
a tortoise shell cat half stretching,
half yawning in the entrance,
incense sticks allowing lazy spirals of odor
to penetrate languid air,
a golden figure half reclining, half smiling
in the dusk

I'll watch the candles burn
and fill the alcove
with the self-same glow
you could apprehend in your heart.

Vainly,
between curling leaves
and young shoots,
the sun will assert authority over a dogged sightseer
who, disposed to go indoors for a meal,
won't feel obliged to surrender to haste
or the calls of vendors to purchase essentials

or trinkets that have no more value
than a poem contemplating the deeds
of a faceless servant long ago:

earth red buckets full of white rice,
capsicum chipped
and dried on the sideboard . . .

after a hard day's labor
the boatman
who ferries passengers to the far side
of the lake
squats beside his wife ladling portions into a bowl.

Without tiring, in an atmosphere of glue
or floating on misty waters,
he would have crammed the boat
with passengers,
steadying them as they embarked
and acknowledging, yes,
the pagoda jutting into the clouds
would be their destination:

the finest silk embroidered
with spirals resembling tongues of living flame,
an ovoid mirror reflecting an inferno
within reach of a star cluster,
a future maker transporting infants from lachrymose dependence
into simplicity foregoing the need to call for succor.

In full view
of the pavilion overlooking his return journey,

he'd listen in on the conversation
between erudite gentlemen ensconced near his tiller:

"When every visitor kept to the shade
or transported an umbrella
to and from each scenic viewpoint,
I ingested the heat
that could swallow
and leave no trace of entry to the land
that makes no allowance for departure
from the living bird discoverable in sleep

white light, waves
and sheen."

"At the end of the causeway,
linking the pine grove
and the expanse planted with an exotic species,
I knelt toward an orchid
cultivated for perfume filling the senses from earth
to heaven

rows
upon rows stained with goddess's blood."

A foreign dignitary swathed in orange and red
makes her way from the high point above the lakeside
toward a redolent mass,
while bringing to mind the features that should last
in her memory
when she returns home:

30: LOST IN LIGHT

a grey stone carved in the shape
of a guardian standing before the entrance to ethereal dimensions,
intimating that slumber will reveal outstretched wings

a journey forsaking a heart
that bleeds shadow water
into growth that has no movement,
labyrinthine paths keeping her guessing where the end will be—

a high priestess who'll isolate grey skin on the nape
and restore its vitality,
eradicate eye soreness,
renew farsightedness

with oracular vision,
see the point healthy tissue becomes rogue
and stymie its rebellion against cloudlessness.

An observer, distant
from the pores
on her skin,
keeps an eye on the colorful figure dropping petals
from the zig zag path

when the midday sun scours the rooftops
and burnishes foliage
upturned to face the harbinger
of greenery,
wonders what her descendent will evoke
when he enters acreage sustained in the unending passage
from her time
to his
and the uninterrupted return from him to her:

30: LOST IN LIGHT

orange carp in the brown water
close to the surface,
an old willow reflected under the arch

perceive the contrasts of summer
and hope they won't disappear
in a blur
when asked to exit the gardens
at the day's end.

31
Sensitivity

I recognize the scent—

lemon
and spice originating from an exotic species

footsteps, the fall of a leaf

am I ready?

A wayward star may end it all before it begins,
a witch confess
I can never bear a child

a rare bird flutter out of sight,
the moon highlight the stain on my cuff

will the moment be right?

A snapped twig may alert woodland creatures
to my approach,
a stumble trepidation

31: SENSITIVITY

blood on a feather draw attention to my heart,
a note on a stringed instrument anticipation

here she is.

An eager touch will dispel the mood,
persuasion interrupt the breath between us,
a trembling lip betray doubt

do you know why I have sent for you?

Prelude to abandonment—

heat transferred backwards and forwards,
air from my air
and taste from your taste

an apple as a gift

do the words really make sense?

Way down the valley

flowers
with bruised petals,
some yet to bloom

31: SENSITIVITY

a glade where one and one only will abide

can you read my thoughts?

Rushes by the pond cease to move,
a frog precedes to croak but stills itself

eyelashes float on your lids

have you anything to say?

I'll share a long-held secret
always withheld:

light on your cheek reflects a distant galaxy,
the pulse in your throat a thrush's heart
in winter rest,
the patch of skin above your breasts
the expanse wherein I make believe
all my troubles will cease

still,
sweet water

no end the depths I have fallen into.

32

Forever

I couldn't count
how many times I've stood on this hill
and watched winged things
of light and clouds race past,
as my father
and his father before,
concentrating on things
for their own sake

a leap far
as an outstretched arm
and the delicate balance on air.

I'll repeat my aim to fly on the wind
with little to remind me
of long loving looks, moist lashes
and peony scent tasted on the first night,
further than the heart's call for someone I knew,
the sound where fish never surface
and the moon's orbit

meld a somnolent voice
with living tissue,
a part of me in it,
a part of it in me

32: FOREVER

extract nutriment from another form of life—

ingrained crust,
fibrous nodes
and blanched vitals

chew at stalks and gnaw at green shoots—

the serrated edge
on edge,
hot chaff and blue skies

in the shadow of a form above,
let it hold me
in its palm and stroke my wings,
with a gentle lift,
emulate height instanced in prayer:

"Allow me to scrape the sun,
approach one
who never asks why pain is incurable"

as midnight suspends activity,
light shines on my face
and ice edges melt,
swirl around your benign features

forgetful of earth's rotation,
shift from one landscape
to another:

mottled, pale fields, glowing limbs,
ribbons of white and clusters of violet flowers

another . . .

a contemplative who dispenses with ritual:

"Stay for a while and bring what you have
and take what I have—

severance from a terminal dance"

the stranger unconcerned with my presence:

"Antagonism is redundant, yet . . .

listen to a peony unfurl:

the blemish free surface
only one is free to set foot upon

enter salt
in fresh water,
a bubble in salt:

the season's chill

32: FOREVER

no matter how faded the bloom pinned to her blouse,
reminding of your one
and only night, translate mist
into a bruise, aether into bone:

"I want to see you again"

recall the red stain
on her lips spreading to the back
of your throat and dabbling in a hot pond:

"I'm afraid I haven't done this before"

with no one by her side collecting tubers
from the water's edge,
tasting the green tips
full of juice before the dry spell arrives

bittersweet on the tongue,
coarse as they go down

keep you going for a lifetime

land again . . .

33
Out of Sight

I'll imagine how far the eagle flies
to avoid danger

uplift
of wings

follow it over the horizon
until blood running from one lake
to another, but never to the sea,
has dissipated

toward a soft blue tinge
and white center, hoping to touch a rainbow
without admixture in frost

my never having had will have
and never learning certain to know.

I'll enter a garden
where plums turn purple
and rare birds keep notes
of happiness above the clouds

33: OUT OF SIGHT

with an eye fixed on an even higher abode,
neck stretching back
in denial, elevate
where the egret's nest has been abandoned
and reminiscence born before I was born
translates shadow language into my native tongue:

"Even where there's clear sky over a range,
amber light between each summit,
you'll find the shaman who'll look under the skin
and tell why your heart quails:

an eyeball retreating to the back
of the skull,
skin drained of blood, smell of old leaves

the chill only a lizard skin will feel."

What if I empty emptiness of emptiness
and stoke inert fires into life?

Will I forget I must suffer the consequences
of being made of the same stuff
as the cripple next door,
entertain an immortal
who'll brush pollen from my lids,
whiten every trace
of night still lingering on my nape
and blow mildest air
to dry the last drop
on my pate

33: OUT OF SIGHT

a ranunculus revealing its calyx,
eschewing a bruise,
fragrance mimicking altar scent
before petals close

an inebriated head above the sun
in love with a standalone god,
swirling in placid streams,
clear water nourishing the roots

who'll open the transparent skylight,
tell how perfect the view, lustrous the strings,
desirous the lips speaking of other worldly environs

whose incumbents will resist an intruder's empty headedness,
retreat even further
where the earth cannot deliver into heavens abode?

34
Intuition

I'll plant the moon on the mountainside,
uncovering virulent growth seductive to an eye

flowers giving off a sick odor will open in luminance,
tendrils coil a ray

each leaf, striated
and bright green, easy to avoid

only a fool exposed to a predator
will ingest it

split open a trunk, allow the sap
to gush out
and mingle tears
with life proceeding from the earth,
but the tree will die
and every insect
in its umbra
submit to the deluge

wash weed hanging from the rocks with the same current
that laps against the stars,

injecting heat into its scant reason
to survive

the rock will split and engulf each strand

with the temerity of a goddess,
blend wild thyme and blood,
saturating each
and every cloud

stand in a downpour
and flood an iris opening toward a rainbow

on the edge of a precipice,
sink into your heart,
know how you approach Heaven
when you sleep
on star filled nights

where only you abide

the soft,
sweet, silent space

smother a wee bird that hops on one foot

or,
watching the red mark appear on my cornea,
select a white blossom
and protect it in ice

34: INTUITION

where the snow accumulates in clefts,
take the downhill path

the sky blue,
morning song clear,
mist dissipating in the foothills

accompany the river, taking sips from a ladle
until I reach your door:

"At long last,
I'm so pleased

a lovely,
lovely present

would you care to fix a tile on the roof,
pull my bed to the window and attend to my leg

I'm sorry,
you couldn't have known

broken
in two places
when wind toppled the pine."

35

A Warm Heart

A source between darkness
and everything that counters it,
where no other can be

an oh partitioned from the last digit
that counts back
to a similar naught preceding the first,
who, consequent to an appearance
far from the end
as the beginning,
shifts perspective to my delight
for its presence,
adulation for the face that loves to see it,
ascribing origin to the utterance:

"Burning out as poppy blooms grow
and you flourish."

Morning illuminates the hair under her lid,
the bubble between her lips
and the crack on her cheek

on the chance
of meeting a goddess,
relinquishing the escutcheons drawn

35: A WARM HEART

from the backwaters of human aspiration,
I'll rise to the crown gilding her finest feature—

the mole in the parting
of her white hair:

alone,
so far away from another likeness,
emptying to points out there
as if stranded and unreachable.

The tree withers,
earth cracks under intense surveillance,
mercury breaks through
and splashes the apex to the nadir

before sleep,
I'll use dishwater to help preserve the one succulent
left from my collection
and, if my ducts fill to the brim,
use every tear to replenish moisture
in the canal winding by the orchard:

not only
with the way of the moon
but beneath the song you shared with your sister
when she held a startled rabbit,
not only shimmering on the puddle
left after the storm
but awake
as day when every pore is closed at midnight.

35: A WARM HEART

An isolated hut
above the smog line receives a message
from an interested purchaser in the city,
the view outside turns from dark
to light grey,
the wires hum

an occupant watches it expand
until ice reflects with the same intensity
a ray streaming through an absence
of repulsion:

a new era withheld
until black spores will die before they breed,
the chart depicting hundreds
only show one.

The dank room,
normally left to the rats,
brightens after the scrub outside the window
is cleared

I'll tie thread to broken glass
and let it twirl

blue,
red and yellow flickering against the wall

walk up a garden path

every flower opening toward the South.

36
Gloom

The flicker against the ceiling:

so
you would have me accept the path next to my boundary
should be covered with a new outhouse blocking the sunlight
on my vegetable patch,
the throughway shared for over a century
used for your benefit at the expense of the wellbeing of others.
How will the old man who lives at the end of the lane,
admittedly at the grace of the neighbors,
be able to reach his shack if you erect your dream house

aren't you satisfied with what you already own?

The thrumming in my ear:

leave the door open
and ponder the extent of his ambitions,
how the rays bend back into their own emanation,
windows overlook the spot where blades grow
and exposed air illuminates circles on powdered wings:

36: GLOOM

"If I could just increase
I won't have to smell his rotten cabbages
or taste the scent
of cauliflower flower
on the back
of my throat."

An ache
in a dry well:

"I'll open his forehead
and take ownership
of his thoughts,
replacing them with my own:

'I have syringed life from a swollen egg and gainsaid heaven

do what he asks of you next door.'"

Ever decreasing circles:

"I'll fill his pond
with manure
and carve initials
in the temple behind his brain."

Settling on my arm:

36: GLOOM

"I'll cut through the roots
that feed his useless flights
into the clouds."

Drinking deeply:

"I'll compel him to coin sentences in ordure
and words from bleeding teeth,
dot the i's with mucus
and parenthesize ellipsis
with a ground down pencil lead:

silken pullets verse night with no head,
rhubarb plucked out of season and fed to the fishes,
the spike mange flitting and courting dewdrops
in solemnity to the spread of vermin through sewers."

The black bits

in jelly:

a butterfly . . .

"I'll seep into bone,
disturb his marrow, push to the left
or to the right . . .

has landed . . ."

36: GLOOM

"Open and shut glutinous jowl,
twist epiglottis, nephritic spasm . . ."

on white flesh . . .

"Crush him . . ."

before lifting into the blue

and will never return
until blood turns light as wind
and the heart cedes rhythm to wing tips.

37

A Reason to Remain

I see her in the window.

After a hard day's work
she looks at the flowers
and wonders how to arrange them—

a large blue surrounded by white, red
or leaves to go with the curtain pulled back
to let in afternoon light,
on the wall
a picture catching their reflection—

two children
and a husband who works far off
but comes home
when time and money permit.

When the old clock on the mantel strikes the hour
she'll resume
where she left off—

feeding the goldfish, straightening bedspreads
and preparing the evening meal
with herbs raised from seedlings

37: A REASON TO REMAIN

occasionally,
the sprinkles land on my side.

Not that I don't do the same,
or she is unable to lead the many
out of conflict,
but for the moment
her identity is centered in tending to bruises
and checking whether a smile is shallow or real

with a tried and tested pattern,
distributing vitality to the organs and limbs

an altar lit up with candles,
a native plant in the corner,
a wind chime beyond the door.

No one shall break the bonds
between all
who belong under her roof,
a stray
will not go unfed
nor the moon pour into an infant's eye

a mirror tilted toward the hall,
cold deflected from the smallest room.

She enters her garden,
selects an iris and hurries inside

37: A REASON TO REMAIN

later,
I see it propped on the sill awaiting an arrangement
that will transform empty space
into a lift under her heart and a wish

someday, someone like her
will help me choose a color
to go with a crumbling fireplace
and charred wood.

38

At Opposite Ends

You'll put sugar in your tea
and I'll drink it straight from the urn

one hand will grab the base,
another
the handle.

"Look through the window—
angular light hits exposed ends or increases
from blades of grass
still wet from the shower."

"Pretend the tea we're drinking
will warm the flower
at the back
of our throats."

You'll appear in vitreous reflections,
I'll stand behind the curtains.

"Until every curve can be calculated
to unfold at the same speed

38: AT OPPOSITE ENDS

as an identical chimera between our eyes,
blacken the air around a single petal."

"Press your forehead against the pane
and allow the cold
to enter

each drop resonates with a tear."

A rift
in the clouds
will brighten your cheekbones
while my face will remain in shadow.

"Lighter than air in lungs that draw down
from high altitudes,
white as cheeks kissed by foreign lips,
the banners lift with tumultuous cheers."

"Where broken bones litter entry
to vestibules made out of age old meat and carapace,
we scrape the earth
to make a hole,
embed our hearts far as we can
from the machinations above."

A sentient being.

"A gust
will bring more rain, reach the lee

38: AT OPPOSITE ENDS

of a trunk
and feelers retreat into a moist casing."

"With each drop, momentarily,
alone,
until joining the puddles on the ground,
an insignificant feeler locates one of its kind."

Unlike the present alive
and healthy
where you find solace,
a recluse born with the sun in the night sky
will count to the heart formed out of the rhythm
of another counted back to.

"Breasts firm against a cotton shawl,
quick fingers harvesting blossoms

a fork
in a branch

to the left—
grey bark,
to the right—a tiny bud

a sprinkling of white powder and fertile lineage,
nurturing the next generation in lands
that will never see poverty."

38: AT OPPOSITE ENDS

"Even though the wind
has penetrated moisture lining secret joints
yet to find pleasure
in running,
a figure will gaze
to the cloud on the horizon:

'A ghostly calm will fog my brow,
tepid streams wash my ears
and I'll hear the creak
of lower organs receiving the impetus to fly.'

Even though trickles of sweat moisten seeds
enabling them to flourish,
every prayer offered to the moon's aura
will displace heat bearing on exposed skin:

'I'll remember the sea breaking on shores redolent
with fruit,
mountain tops ablaze,
dust whirling in orbit.'

Even though the strength in one limb
is adequate,
every calling to act in a manner befitting a great warrior
will be questioned:

'I'll make do with windblown seed,
absorb nutriment
from the fly on my shoulder

38: AT OPPOSITE ENDS

prefer,
despite the fact my feet have pads for walking,
nails are hard
and sprout like plants in a shadow,
not to move.'"

Although you'll emphasize the impact of solar winds
on passing travelers
and bright eyes,
while I'll cultivate words of ancient derivation
in a trance that precedes their origin,
we still meet
to talk about what I did yesterday
and what you will do tomorrow

yet,
avoid committing to the next meeting
and the thought we don't particularly care
for the language the other uses
to persist in their calling.

39

Forgetfulness

A light filled glade and rainbow hues are out of my reach . . .

walk in the park instead

the neighbor's dog blocking the path . . .

hold off until it is called home

the licensed grocer,
certain anyone who spends time
trying to find where rivers meet the ocean
and taste freshwater mingling with salt
is only draining the resources
of the hardworking,
lifts a bottle
with the thought of parting the waters that sustain me . . .

until the moment subsides,
pause at the curb
and count the feathers on a blackbird

unrequited spring yet to tinge a bud
with yellow . . .

39: FORGETFULNESS

meld autumn's chill
and damp under my eyelids

iron railings,
headstones
and the odor of earth clinging to my palate . . .

arrest the urge to swig from a brown bottle
and cancel every color
that comes in from the sea

half-light seeking out hidden places,
earth rising to meet the highest point . . .

prick your finger with a thorn
and watch the tip redden without effort

rime on living,
glistening skin
the same as dripping from a cadaver . . .

lift low light into light above the skull

burnt husks littered upon stone,
a severed finger upon the marble,
drums pounding in haze . . .

temper a lion's drive
to claw from captivity,

39: FORGETFULNESS

impede a merchant's zest to excite
with oil crushed from rose hips,
even guide the stars
and steer elemental forces through marrow

a gate carved in radiant blue . . .

funnel determination
to spread beyond your father's dominion
which, too, plundered the heart
and gave it back with a notch

annihilation . . .

find an out of the way corner looking onto a row
of weeds,
thistles
and scraps blown in
from rubbish bins that line the cul de sac

charred skin,
souvenir of the day's rout,
wrapped around my forehead . . .

excise all traces
of foreign descent

the smell
of burning leaves
from the fire the caretaker built near the hedge . . .

39: FORGETFULNESS

with a wet finger,
erase the initial scraped into the woodwork
when you thought everything you produced
would last no longer
than a lifetime

the streetwise vendor,
who approaches from the west,
offering a simple range—

tape and bird whistles,
pencils and notepads:

"I haven't had any interest
in anything of mine today."

"Never mind, a couple of these will do . . ."

wrap a white band around your finger

draw high clouds on paper

taste blue light between the leaves.

40
Release

What gives you the right to criticize?
Have you plunged
where intoxicated revelers crave more
to assuage their thirst
or risen where gods pour nectar on swollen tongues?
On softened footfall would you creep through the ages
in search of your affliction?
I think not.
Like the rest in this wretched street,
unconcerned with the eternal essence
invisible to brain matter—
all *they* think exists,
you ply the surface.
Have you any idea
how deeply eggshell jam clings to the asylum
and the gaze of love
which could liberate it?

It infuriates me how thieves crawl
on cold nights,
people leave their rubbish in walkways
and an oaf lounges against an entrance.

If I had my way
I'd clear the lot of them
with a broom or write their names
in a register bound for no man's land.

40: RELEASE

"Are you any different?

The other day you broke a neighbor's fence
and didn't tell him, kicked his dog
because it was barking too loud
and swore at a public official
because the fine you were meant to pay
was overdue,
incurring another penalty.

The malodorous and intentionally corrupt aside,
can we say we fail,
our ambitions get in the road
of compassion
and pet projects outweigh the demand
to look at another's suffering.

You can't complain

you are doing what you want to do
and are indebted to others to support you,
most probably
they say, unfairly

you have nourishment to keep you alive,
a bed to sleep in
and a roof over your head to keep out the rain

so,
the next time when I refuse to take up your script,
you won't abuse me

40: RELEASE

you'll remember you write primarily for your own interest
without my approval motivating you
to quaff cinnabar flecks in jade liqueur."

Really, you do value my judgement

a lot can be gained
from a butterfly's wing fluttering over the wall
and dipping with the wind.

Squashed beneath a boot of rage,
my time is at an end

I flew for no reason
than to invest a fragile beauty
in movement,
giving the transitory a new lease,
annihilated for fear of being torn from corporeality
and requested to exit the last room.

On your way out,
I'll hold the door open
and promise never to rile you

wait,
I'll flick the dust off your shoulder
and take back the bundle I expected you to read

scrape frost
from the window

40: RELEASE

in the distance an old man supported by a stick,
eggshells and yolk

a pumpkin squashed against the curb,
an official delivering letters as usual

if she has one for me,
I'll mention how moist the air becomes
when grey clouds appear on the horizon

she should hurry
to avoid being wet,
her job must involve a lot of toil

she's coming my way,
approaching the letter box

ice melting on the path

most probably another overdue bill,
a rejection slip
or an advertisement for a home improvement scheme

a flickering streetlight

no, she didn't put one in

40: RELEASE

now,
I have only to put up with the neighbor's dog
and loneliness.

41
Diminution

The sparrows nest crushed by the falling tree

too late to arrest the fledglings rolling into the stream,
stop the veranda collapsing

every window smashed,
manuscript scattered in the mud,
rain gurgling in the pipes

ink washed out,
grey and blue mingling white seeping into blue

unreadable.

A mindless whirl dumping weight onto fragile stems,
need to be where you were never meant to stand,
movement beyond the stagnant
and otiose?

Step into vulgarity and drunkenness,
abandon good taste, make do with apple peelings,
husks and green potatoes

41: DIMINUTION

collect as many ants as stars
and smear them over my lids,
break their backs
and let the contents stop me
from catching sight of summer

the pell-mell drop to the floor
when thunder hits the roof?

Hold wet bodies into the light
and thank the Heavens
it wasn't my head in their stead,
throw them into the blue
and revive a portion of blood
until it spreads to the extremities

a solar flare touching the beat in shadow,
dew drops staining white noise

catch their offspring
who'll remember the same warm hands?

As they fall
to my side

steeped earth smelling of urine,
the neighbor's yearling bleating for her to wake up

never again presume the heat under their wings,
the raw need to escape

41: DIMINUTION

would cancel the pull
to the rocks beneath?

Rub the tears and focus on the wellspring
as if the storm had never occurred
and taste the same flow
as if it had never been born until now:

the solitary cloud brooding all afternoon,
an old cat stretched out on the shed,
the eternal wish
I could stand forever
where nothing ever impinges,
the day drains all focus upon effort
and I am not required
to struggle with your desire
to make me answer your clamoring for attention
on such a lazy day?

Boil the mush, flatten it and make new paper

I can always recover a word
or an idea as long as I can breathe,
hold a pen and evince the secret undertones
which always seem to appear no matter how I fare

reconstruct where I left off:

a spent force:

41: DIMINUTION

finders keepers,
mine not yours

two healthy hands:

ability to clasp them in gratitude
easily as it is to hold a brush,
sharpen a pencil
and draw a design
for a prayer room that can hold gardening implements

the missing piece
you'd sacrifice a wealth of mortal treasures
to recover:

the umpteenth time I asked Heaven
to eliminate the crying over the hedge

two legs:

one that can push an antiquated spirit level
from out under the wreckage
and the other
hold steady for balance

coincidence:

every odor,
every rumble,

41: DIMINUTION

every flash delineating tangled branches
motivating you to cling to the next
as if I were the author

a steady,
good arm:

until twilight,
hammering nails in boards
to cover the hole in the fence

when everyone goes indoors,
throwing back the precious artefact your son left over my side
with an end to warding off the assaults from demons
he knew lurked at the end of the garden,
but complemented the altar I had in mind
to build in the shade of the now fallen tree

and raise my hopes to the cosmos.

42

Ascension

On the afternoon
I heard of your accident
I wanted to raise my gaze into the clouds
and pretend,
like the rain,
I could descend to the earth
and nourish every bloom and creature
that scurries to avoid being drenched,
with the same intensity
as a goddess
from realms transcending the broken eggshell
still beating within,
blow teardrops to Orion
and identify the blood beneath your feet
with a river flowing to a moonlit inlet
and the expanse that preceded entry
into the life of hurt,
as midnight envelops receding eyesight
and teeth daring not to move
lest they betray pain,
lift the veil and light up your features:

a ray penetrating to the petal
in the hedge,
bathing it until it glows

42: ASCENSION

an unexpected visitant evoking the highest sentiment,
overcoming shock and the fear you may disappear
in a whirlpool unconstrained by love

a wandering star with the license
to guide a wayfarer to safety,
following tracks preordained from when it began

yet,
as you may have found,
I am ineffectual as scent sprinkled on briar rose
and the best I can do is to say,
"What a fine fellow he was," respectfully,
to the groundsman who shifts loam
from one plot to another,
show an old photograph
of a friendly smile to the boy delivering leaflets
to the neighbor

taking care not to smudge the paper,
hand your poems
to the local school master
who would publish imaginative meter
on his day off.

43

A Legitimate Request

For too long the water leaking from our pipes has been tainted.
Each drop tastes as if green algae clouds the source and dirt bears down upon the flow.
In mid-afternoon heat
mosquitoes hover above the surface and lay eggs at will

succulents steep
in grey desire to retreat.

Not only is health in jeopardy
but visitors are dismayed by the negligence

we dig new channels but are defeated
by the immensity of the task.

Invocation beyond the world remained unanswered
and the old monk
who buries the dead ceased to care

wounds must be treated regardless.

43: A LEGITIMATE REQUEST

A spring bubbles to the center where white narcissi bloom,
a cupful will quench a traveler's thirst
and wash a baby clean, idle beauties peer at their reflection

it augurs regret to flourish while others suffer the indignity
of privation

no prognostication militates against change.

Although you are embittered by an attack from subversive elements,
finances are stretched to their limits and many exigencies press
on your attention,
make amends,
refresh our conduits and palates

drain every stinking pond.

It is in the interest of the harmony of the populace as a whole
to attend to our demands
for, without the support of even the lowliest of residents,
the capacity to deal with the terrors that beset us will be weaker.

A stagnant heart will refuse to beat in time

with a resolution

to protect its homeland.

44

A Way Out of Hell

I prize open the shell, anticipate white flesh,
sauce and wine

nothing more exquisite
than liquid swirling under my nose

dream of faraway places
where plump fingers caressed fruit
from the vine,
pressed it between her thighs,
succumbed to the bidding of a master
and lay in the hay,
slipping below his knees

ancient odor of heat
and surrender,
a red moon in her mouth

emptied playthings
out of the old box kept under her bed
and placed the baby inside,
reaching well beyond heartbroken tears

44: A WAY OUT OF HELL

dawn on the other side

crept through the rain in search of an eviscerated stallion
that clogs the airways,
concocting a lotion
to smear under the nose of the dead

an uncanny twist on her lips

sprinkled eye fluid
on suitors growing to twice their normal size,
at the exhortation
of a widow imparting tales of heinous aftereffects
and scandalized by indecency,
finding herself in the marketplace
to burn
where pigeons catch fire and ignite the town

smoke curling away with lewd sighs

enclose abundant light,
restoring culture from the rubble

enlightened seers with necks like candles,
smitten by words executed
with a nib flicked this way and that,
captivating eternal desire
to comprehend the pulse of repletion
and worship treasuring the point humanity looks outward
toward the one, flickering beyond her headstone,
making each planetary orb sing

44: A WAY OUT OF HELL

instead,
forgo your evening meal
and close the shell

stomp on it
until it shatters

the contents spread across the floor.

45

A Common Interest

It is beyond my capacity to digest the meaning of every saying
without the assistance of a friend who has studied the appropriate literature
for years. On the other hand, he has difficulty in seeing clearly,
so I can point out the correct phrases in their order. Another friend,
whom I don't see too often, likes to take part in our discussion.
It helps him to reach conclusions he could never reach on his own.

We shall meet in the room at the back of the Community Hall
where they store brooms and such like. We will study
for an hour before the sun sets. The passage, this time,
will be from the Book of Changes Hexagram 45:

"A king will approach his temple."

Can you remember the official who came by the other day—
the short man with the horn-rimmed spectacles? Well,
his proposal is for a new building where this one stands

light and vision beyond his immediate interests
will exemplify the facility where adherents of all creeds
will be welcome

45: A COMMON INTEREST

all manner of activities, including ours, granted extra room

a place for worship,
somewhere for collectors to show precious items,
a compassionate heart to help people through trauma,
residents to express anger at inordinate decisions

a refuge for children threatened by unhealthy advances.

He is, at this moment, widening the road

it will bring more people to the area
and some who may be interested in joining our group.
Who knows, we may even attract a scholar
who could plumb the wisdom of the Yi
and set us free from unenlightened contemplation.

"It is advantageous to meet with a great man.
Rendering offerings will ensure good fortune."

We shouldn't hesitate
in contacting a prestigious school now

we could invite someone with high credentials
to take part in a discussion.

We must be prepared to clean our clothes,
though,
and bring out that old bottle of wine stored for special occasions.

45: A COMMON INTEREST

We could send some notes

the importance of disseminating ideas
to even the lowliest of citizens should suffice.

"Having a goal will be advantageous."

Whatever is born out of the image
will in turn be presented to an audience
who'll feel they've been drawn together
in the one will and the one momentum

they'll give up their time to help complete the project.

"The superior man hones his weapons
in order to meet the unexpected."

Be careful on your way home
because we will separate
and go our different ways

already
the colors of the day are fading

despite the development lights have yet to be installed.

45: A COMMON INTEREST

Although we have found the meanings in words
we must live them out
for the joy in each other's company,
overflowing
into the night, could leave us vulnerable
to danger impinging on high hopes
and star filled eyes.

46

As Far as I Can Go

No mundane sound could emulate,
"You were with me, tasting midnight
before light identified with a solar flare,
felt the cut
that separated a thrush's outpouring from a healthy ear,
yet regained composure
after the hummingbird tipped over.

An ocelot will claw onto a ledge
that smells of fear
and a gnat savor leaves rotting against a north facing wall
where it can expand its kind."

Ink will splash
while attempting to record the flight
intent on keeping up
with one who could discover the source of flight.

As wind beats down the fence
between black stubble and the well-worn track
and the shadow clings to every square inch
of skin,
charisma accrues like the ray from the furthest star,
"I have much to give you."

46: AS FAR AS I CAN GO

Clouds on the horizon couldn't compare
with one mixed with blood and sugar
when grass effects a temperate green,
the pigeon deeper grey
and brains a tinge
of pink.

Oil scented with spice
and flowers spread over loving couples
will not deter the breath
from taking in frozen mist on a white peak
or the heart daring to abide in a garden,
a burning stick thrust into a stream
obscure a handful of snow presented as a gift
or a blossom disappearing into the mass
of color
when the tree bursts into spring.

Although you may seem an eon away
from a rising eye,
detachment won't increase beyond the arc
between this life
and the one to come,
a limpid interior will make the sun's rays clear

I'll recall you over my shoulder
linking your overarching vision
with my unsteady hand,
surpassing what I can see:

melilotus in bloom,
a tumbling rill
and gentle slope

46: AS FAR AS I CAN GO

one dressed in blue
with hems of yellow,
who turns a twig
to inspect the bruises on its underside,
and, still holding it despite its flaws,
raises his face

(or her lucid eyes)

"I'll vouch for you when eternity calls."

47

Sorrow

In the graveyard close to an aching forehead
and the drop in temperature
as the north wind follows the same pattern it has for millennia,
I'll tell of rouge on a nose
when he acted in a play
our locally esteemed director guessed
would signify the full weight
of all he had in mind
to embody like a rotten plum:

an animal tunneling toward an exit
awash with flood from the mountains,
an escapee cringing before the palace guard located him
and returned him to a cage,
in the imprint of a hoof
an insect fluttering in the shade of another coming down

the circuitous route
to reach the sea, bypassing the acrid storm water drains
that never flush out

cold lips of a fish.

47: SORROW

I shouldn't forget to mention
as he gulped the brine
he would have recalled that when the tide closes over
and the weed wraps around the windpipe,
the blue in the waves,
the turquoise near to the surface
and the amber filtering beneath his feet
would not be eradicated
if he loved as he did
when his sister showed him her coloring book:

a butterfly landing on a stalk,
examining every segment,
counting the rings on its wings

unbeknownst to the girl he hoped to woo,
imagining her face
in the eyes gazing toward the purple range

when it flew off, wishing her the adulation
for all things spirited
and free

it would,
he expected, visit realms
where only the light-hearted would venture:

"What brings you here,
so far away
from your usual abode

47: SORROW

did the scent of a blind goddess tempt you to cross
and feast on her contents,
the tones of ancient lovemaking erase memory?"

Above the earth unravelling silk
and letting it trail behind

sometimes it will catch on a tooth,
a nail
or a fingertip

but it'll still pull and continue

there is no one who'll stop it

it'll go on past the shimmering cliffs,
the glittering range and pink tinged waterfall
till no one else can emulate the journey . . .

the moon hanging on a thread—

an infant's face so unreachable
it can't be made to appear at the will
of a mother's love,
so easily marked cannot be touched,
only nourish a heart purified of an excessive urge
to display it around the torso

47: SORROW

mellowing the glare that preceded,
silhouetting the steps leading upward,
presaging a torturous climb from a baser than corrupt entity
that would swallow it whole . . .

a mallard drifting on duckweed pond—

so full of titbits
and unnecessary food thrown from the bank,
it wouldn't be able to rise above the treetops,
let alone lift into the sunset

with the compassion of one,
who feels that any gesture of kindness
earns a favor from an otherworldly protector,
he'd reach into his pocket
and pull out another handful
of rice crackers and pumpkin seed.

As we gather in a clump
while the drops trickle down our necks,
keeping our finger
on the passage which suggests a jonquil will grow
on the roughest ground,
throwing the last sod into the hole,
I'll say my last piece about a young man
whose conviction to deny the soft fall of hair on his chest
for a life in the priesthood
only reinforced our inkling that it wasn't meant to be:

47: SORROW

one morning
to mend a hole in the suit borrowed from the neighbor,
one hour to accompany a parent past the playground
we tumbled in,
one minute to scrutinize each face
and see who cared the most,
a second to bury his smile

one rain drenched instant
to let on how much you know,
but how little you can say.

48
Wellspring

In a neighboring village the water supply is generous
for they abut South Mountain
high enough for ice and snow.

Numerous rills trickle to the base and seep underground,
soil is moist
and crumbles in your fist

light often shines on puddles.

Some grow vegetables,
a few cultivate flowers
and fruit

every garden flourishing,
each stall an abundance
of green, red and yellow.

An old pipe empties into a lane

on days
when heat penetrates the deepest sediment

48: WELLSPRING

children swallow mouthfuls,
a rook ruffles her feathers,
workers returning from night duty wash shadows
from their eyes, grit under the fingernails

allow the fluid
cold
and unimpeded splash on stone.

Concerned citizens protest development
with the potential to contaminate streams
and leach into the life force beneath their feet,
words of encouragement
are addressed to representatives
who support conservation of resources.

We hope to visit our friends
and taste the clarity, sniff the air,
expect the chill and swirl our fingers
in the pools.

For ages
a stone well has served the town square

it is sworn
if the night is clear and one peers from the right angle
a star will reflect on the surface,
a coin thrown in sound loud
as a wave on rocks

48: WELLSPRING

with a hand cupped over one ear
a tune the ancients remembered in their dreams
float up from the depths:

Everyone can quench their thirst,
enjoy the source,
discover heartache in a word,
the split second coming to know one's lifelong partner
in a look

the timeliness in its flow.

No one need be reluctant

a scholar with a furrowed brow,
an onlooker standing above

a simple homebody with a story to tell.

49
A New Start

One chilly morning,
with the fire crackling in the hearth,
you got round to telling me
why you thought it appropriate to visit,
that it was important we sat down for a chat

for, in your words,
"I haven't many people to tell what I really, deeply believe,
who won't think I am a fool
or I've lost my mind somehow.

My stupid neighbor decided to instigate a feud:

'It was you who spread filth over the pathways.'

I was bound to retaliate:

'Must you cough so loudly,
allow the ashes
from your bonfire blow over the fence

do you always have to scold your son
and hit your wife

49: A NEW START

punctuate every utterance
with a curse,
shake your fist after I ask you to control yourself?'

The diseased kids in the old hostel,
as far as I was concerned
like the fool next door,
were caught up in their own pact
with misery

growth
on the kidneys the result
of the stuff they swigged out of brown bottles,
poison their mother would feed them

too bad they don't have the wherewithal
to pull themselves out of it.

To an equally determined figure sitting upright,
pulling back the clouds

tepid streams
and blue tinged groves, scaling heights

I emphasized the futility
of raising his heart
into a verdant acre,
plucking the fruit:

49: A NEW START

'Not one iota of evidence, nothing specific, nothing
that could be taken as corroborating the existence
of any being outside the structures
that makes up natural life.

Hear the raindrop on the leaf resonating in time
with the dance upon our own skin

the drumbeat of centuries alone
is enough.

See the child laugh,
isn't that enough to join in with him?

Feel the lover,
her warmth and caress

taste her sweat,
entangle yourself in her arms.

There is no need to go beyond this,
no need
to create another to make it worthwhile,
no need to address otherness
as if we need it

no need at all.'

49: A NEW START

Then, at a local hostelry,
sitting outside with a tasty drink in my hand:

'You will perish
with no one to care'

alone,
consigned to a pauper's grave
where each blade will cover and leave no trace
of rhythm, breath and song

so far back,
an eyeball turned in on itself,
keeping an eye
on drips from dead glands

still in every vein:

'Only that I love to.'

The driest part of rain,
the quickest leap of a snail

a level spirit level
even though the ground slips beneath
at an awkward angle,
a steady temperature even though ice coats the fringe

49: A NEW START

zeal to eradicate communion
with one,
who can judge the point
of entry over the chasm,
challenged by the taste
for clusters hanging beyond the bridge
crossed behind a pointing finger

blossoms full of nectar:

'I have no reason to call on you,
I just love to.'

'You'll have no reason
to call on me, you'll just love to.'

And what of the blisters,
wheals and broken fingerbones

the decaying matter, broken glass
and food scraps

the blue-black heart
that never appears over the horizon,
pumping daily in
and out,
without so much as an inkling why
it never abandons its own lonely nest?

49: A NEW START

Embedded in the skull, the hips or the feet
an illusion
or a memory that turns idyllic nights
into an iceberg jutting into brain matter,
a cruel finger stroking a womb

cold flames, transparent earth,
glistening dust

rose scent clean as effluence,
silence full of an unending stream,
the cacophony silent
as light

taste of water stained with blood,
finger pressing hard against my temple,
indenting the skull

sunlight that shines at night,
sweat that doesn't run

a mother
who borrowed time from a falling rock,
a father denying her succor,
the midwife drinking the fluid
meant to wash me clean

the same bowl used to store winter bulbs
under my bed
tipped out, polished
and placed on the mantle

49: A NEW START

so clean it reflects the scar above my ear.

I could see the idiot next door holding counsel
with an old woman, trying to convince her
of my culpability in crime

I spoke to him later

in the manner, perhaps,
of a lapwing folded up for the night.

In the early hours garbage was dumped
into the stream running by our boundary

carefully,
I picked up every piece and deposited them in a container.

The pavement leading to the woods
was marked with grime

I took to it
with a hard brush.

A blowfly will land on a swathe
of rags, children's foot sores are swollen
by lack of attention

49: A NEW START

sooner than later,
I'll write an application volunteering my services
at the hostel

do you know of anyone who can give me a reference?"

50
A Meal for One

I read it is not appropriate to eat snow.

What if fallen
without a hint
of wind,
hasn't touched anything except a cloud
and pockets of air never breathed in

the last drops landing on my tongue?

Would it refresh my temper,
embed reminiscence
in ocular nerves
that could pry a little deeper?

Do you suppose a number
of flakes could settle on my brow
until numbness envelops the mist
between silken hair falling on her nape
and moisture under an eyelid,
light up the having happened,
but obscured,
once in a lifetime moment knowing the wrong path:

50: A MEAL FOR ONE

her preference for inch long whips
than a finger across the spine,
an afternoon stroll
that'd take an hour looking at bird's nests
and butterfly's wings over in a minute

a broken bone
than a boyish grin,
the caress finding nothingness in hot breath brushed aside?

What if I use it for soup prepared with fresh vegetables
washed in a stream equally as pure,
salt less with only a touch
of pepper prepared in a glass bottom bowl?

When steam rises and bubbles pop,
would it sustain my journey into the mountains

when the moon hides behind red gauze
and I need to tell which pass to enter,
evoke centuries old odors

vengeance still simmering beneath wanton looks:

a child wrenched from her mother's side

somewhat like the toy
she owned,
a pumpkin seed on a string?

50: A MEAL FOR ONE

What had he eaten before,
this adventurer
into foreign lands,
who breathed in the aroma like *his* ancestor?

Horse's blood, roast femur
and acid bulbs torn from a neighbor's patch?

Forgotten
behind immobile dynasties fraught with dementia:

each night the crow calling for a black mate
to share leftovers of a feast

the grit under his lid preventing him
from looking into the back of their eyes,
catching the color of the remains
they were pecking at:

his ancestor
beside a swollen river
with her teeth on the ground,
a few bandits standing by cooking their evening meal:

nipples of a fox,
eye of rat,
an earlobe cut from the prettiest victim
of the day's rout

50: A MEAL FOR ONE

the scent filling his head,
stinging his eyes,
clouding wet whispers
how much he appreciated each spoonful.

Will the fumes reach the heights, bring rain,
wash my forehead clean?

If taken back to the foothills,
supplementing my meagre rations,
would it warm the soles of my feet
to the brain,
dilute the shadows within the same,
recurring pattern:

a red glow around my face
when after supper I'd want to rest,
watch light on the walls . . .

and she'd have to pierce my ear
and attach a golden ring—
the coil they'd use to bring her to her knees,
marks around my wrist
when she grabbed me after losing a game
of chance

50: A MEAL FOR ONE

inspire a delicious sense
I have arrived where only healthy animals roam,
the lantern always bright
and I can see the footsteps leading up to the girl
I am meant to marry,
but will refuse her hand

walks on lonely trails
more inviting
than the tasty dishes she'll prepare
with condiment
and ingredients stolen from the local shopkeeper?

51
Shock

While sleeping

a knock at the door.

"Who is it?"

The escaped madman with a price on his head

no one

my stupid neighbor.

"Go away."

I have no time to dally with eagerness . . .

bones bleed
in the ocean,
twilight shimmers on the shore,
turtles glide over the reef

51: SHOCK

so what,
you have a new son

the world is already full
of their cries, enough to feed already . . .

scent the foothills
with plum, taste the clouds,
carry me over the threshold
unencumbered by worldly desire

out of reach.

Tap. Tap. Tap.

Is it the same man
or an echo in my slumber?

"What now?"

"Please come."

Cold under my feet

lips a red wound

51: SHOCK

black
then white.

"What do you want of me?"

Black again.

"I need someone to hold him
while I tend to my wife."

"Can't you do it yourself?"

"He has funny legs
and won't lie properly."

The moon the shape
of a lemon,
a tree withering in the gale,
blood
on the floor

black eyes looking up at me.

52
Quietude

I live in the world
but want to die where life begins,
go on but stay in the center

creep toward a fading light, equally
as I would wish to stand
in the sun warming my back

align the morning star
with rays reflecting into my heart

enter interior realms,
secret depths that makes one bend one's knees
and peer inside

a mirror reflecting the same face seen with a thousand eyes,
millennia stretched from the azimuth to the nadir:

when the dust settles
and the shadow seems not to follow the movement
of the sun
a moth flutters in search of a mate,
when he brushes his wing

against hers
they'll stop awhile
entranced by the lazy glow upon their feelers:

a cloudless day, scent of orchid,
the old windmill barely moving

condiments spread
on outstretched cloth,
mangoes sliced in yellow bowls,
elixir drawn from an artefact father would disapprove of
if aware she took it for want
of something more suitable:

white separating a blue swallow from a blue cloud,
a punt moored
to a gnarled root,
a scholar contemplating a ragged scroll:

faintly discernible in ageing ink,
miles and miles
contorted by quakes having lost an impulse
to create a new domain,
a youth ascending a bare face:

I have reached the summit
where the venerable master abides,
hear him reciting that passage he loves:

the drip from the tap
we never get around to repairing,

52: QUIETUDE

the tempo
I recall
when I lay my head on her chest

water in the well so clear
white pebbles can be counted,
the space
between the lining on my jacket
and skin after a bath

navigation
through rays from heaven
still subsisting behind undiscovered wastelands,
a nerve between healed fiber
and bones finding it hard
to get up
after one hundred and fifty years

redolent flowers that don't change places,
skull thick
as ironwood
and amber moons
where distant relatives borrow vitality
from earthbound,
though farsighted inhabitants:

the blinking of a lid
so gentle
I could rest contentedly in the closure,
drifting of a leaf so quiet
it can be heard from Wednesday to Saturday

52: QUIETUDE

marrow on fire
with the sense
one is loved longer than a lifetime.

53

Development

Even though inhaling air redolent
with the scent
of white blossom beneath an ancient tree,
turning toward the land below,
catching sight of a chasm athwart the countryside,
I cannot help watching childhood misdemeanors
as if they occurred yesterday:

a stolen apple,
footprints where every surface had been cleaned thoroughly,
fingers pointing at the wrong eye,
sobs
of denial,
a strangled kitten kicked behind the fence

although I can hear you telling me
that I'll be loved when tides fail
to rise,
never have to delve in worlds
where the night's frigid hours reach my eyelashes
and you'll identify me
from the millions who clamor
for attention,
won't I hear through the candid whispers
her last little sobs and choking for air?

53: DEVELOPMENT

A wayfarer tapping his staff
once for heavenly abundance, twice
for universal appetite for inspiration,
three times for a dragon ascending to the clouds
makes his way into the mountains to visit the goddess
said to know the secrets of a bountiful life.

An ashen look
upon irises, a clock rewound to its full extent,
a tap left to drip:

"Prepare to face the end."

Egg monster broken
in the pristine palace, leaking between shutters
where mommy roams with a blood axe

a shallow bay,
palm trees,
water blue
as cobalt
in a paint box,
white sand stretching along the foreshore

a black spider in a black cave:

the earth's time to spend suspended in itself
without waking up

plums:

53: DEVELOPMENT

edible blue-black seconds
from the earth

juice:

the tang of darkness making clouds swirl inside

rich mixture spread between rows to increase yield,
enliven
where usually no other living thing could subsist,
seep into the levels underlying the warmth
and openness to enable a seed to expand into a shoot:

the tender tips
of an orchid growing in a hothouse,
on the surface of a pond
a lotus flower

each chosen for their capacity to grow
where the stain proceeded from the contaminated earthworks,
the stench emanated from the distillery

how they made you enjoy the aura around the carcass
even though
you may never catch sight
of its gamboling in the fields again.

Through the swirl and roar of one gust after another
the gate bangs against supporting posts,
rain spatters against the wall isolating me

53: DEVELOPMENT

from the memory of drowning
when the deluge encroached upon the earth
and spread to the heavens . . .

I can tap the pane
in the same manner echoing each drop:

"One two three,
one two, one two."

Emptiness smells like dust
on a candle lit by your hand.
Everything you do discerned
like a shadow on the wall.
I pretend you could grow into a seed
where pain finds inception,
blossom into a tree that supports my weight,
hold me forever in the storm.

Your beat
is mine, absorbing distance
with laughter
once you knew I was yours:

a luminous descent wiping away tears,
stroking each tendon stretched before its loving presence

53: DEVELOPMENT

earth red patterns on white rock,
sun baked mice flitting toward a hole
in the back of my brains

long after my ancestor paused to reflect on *his* ill will:

bad smelling winds, an oaken door smashed down,
the baby and mother carried off

held underwater until the bubbles burst

singed meat on a spit,
fat dripping in flames

pink fingertips

however,
appealing to the love of Heaven
that will float in my tears

a word of kindness reaching the stars:

"Come on, don't be afraid.
You're a sweet little cat, aren't you,
although you won't let me touch you?
I've never seen such matted fur
and filthy paws. Where did you come from?
What's that stuff weeping from your eye?

53: DEVELOPMENT

Here

drink some warm milk
and lay by the fire."

54

Vitriol

If I had the capacity
to get under your skin,
collude
with pulse timed with need,
expand into space beyond limits—

the bloated calf, baked offal pie

a hollow where no one can find a way out—

harmonize the red raw tip,
the crimson lake in flood
and fresh meat,
what could I bring forth?

An era that disposed with clammy palms,
fountains splashing dust from the brow

the ripest cluster
a god could espy

54: VITRIOL

chosen from the many
a bough above the cataract's descent?

I
will do what I want:

carve initials in statues
and squeeze nectar from mountain orchids.

I will have
what I want:

the future
in a looking glass, the past
in a flame
and the present between my fingers.

I
will become whatever lengthens tomorrow:

a drop of white on blinding light,
a millisecond
in a minute

luminous flight the day after

left to dry

54: VITRIOL

a dewdrop sparkling in heat,
a snowflake resting on coals

the heart in the head.

I shall write anything
I feel:

the lip sucker's appetite
for running water close to your bones:

"Over the threshold,
carry me"

an egg opening and giving life
to a lupine ghost bound for tasty ligaments

swallowing you whole, smearing clouds
with secrets the universe will want to know:

You are the earth I'll saturate,
the everywhere
I can plumb,
the silence that will open in my presence.

I want to go on
in love with gorged ends,
blood rising and release

54: VITRIOL

far as the craters on the moon,
deep as the creature that swims
illuminated by its own inner light

sing when the fire eliminates the last trace
of every encounter linking me
to your newfound love,
stars that light up an eye swelling with affection

without me,
empty

whistle a merry tune
when the man
of your life falls and breaks his neck.

55
Glory

The dream presaged meeting with powers
that took away birdsong and replaced it
with speech,
every nuance required
to express the dawn executed
with a resounding note
upon note:

"We need more than a morsel
to sustain our day,
more than a memory to find
from where the next thing
that enthuses us will arrive

we'll combine effort
to accomplish everything one can't do alone
and, as late-night images appear darkly in a shadow,
gather to pronounce the birth of a new-found moment
since we don't realize what preceded it."

Nothing seems to promote an incentive to continue

what with the demeaning way I live.

Breadcrumbs licked from the one plate,
pieces of cheese stored for a week
and grated on the same plate,
the recurring prayer uttered day in and day out:

"Please,
something to write about."

Bright edges,
tinctures
of dark green and a lemon

dust free—

superimposed
on the old

leaves twisted by invisible fingers,
trained to meet the moon's light

when the sourness leaves the back of the throat
a pleasant astringency.

I am getting old,
every step a little more difficult
than a year ago,
the slightest chill works into my marrow

the stain of blue upon a squall,
blue line
on the horizon.

I'll nestle in the dunes

birds wheeling toward the south,
the tide creeping toward my feet

trust,
no matter how near to complete rest,
I am at least able to reach out
and touch a glistening spider's web,
hold out for kindness in the present
although she seems far away
and unconcerned
with shadows passing through dying tissue:

"I'll appease chaos with a kiss,
arrest the decline
where mortals sense expulsion
from the world
and retard the growth of mold
with light apparent beyond the sun."

For the third time this week
I have forgotten the name
I was given,
whether I had a visitor
when the roar of the waves subsided

alone, despite the fact
I think the visitation in love
and joy really happened:

"I chanced a time in furrows
so long they never seemed to end

at least,
far as the thread connecting an ageing lobe
with outer stellar disclosures

the future encapsulated in the beginning
before you happened
in the blink of an eye:

I'll take you
someday."

Once more,
I hope she'll appear when the day blazes at noon,
align my grievance with the morrow
that hasn't felt an inevitability to decrease
or cry
and recite the passage I think I'll remember correctly:

55: GLORY

"I'll extrude dust
from a pearl and tinctures of blood
from a lotus flower,
hold the center aloft
till you step where you're invited

the brittle frame
that could shatter too easily retaining its shape,
inclining toward to a smile."

56
Wayfarer

I'll press flowers in a book to show
I have been to the places where they grow,
arrange leaves in a pattern depicting the trail
that led from one mountain to another and,
when chatter in the hall quietens down
and the lovers next door cease to murmur,
trace on a map the roads that took me
to a temple under an overhanging cliff,
a glade where trees discover heights
in reach of ancient memory
or the river
which plunged into a cavern
before reappearing again on its way to the ocean.

After hearing the chant in the distance
a young man holding an object looked up:

"So,
you're on a journey seeking new wonders.
Here, look at this"

an ordinary buttercup somehow glowing.

56: WAYFARER

Descending from the clouds
an old wayfarer paused:

"I recommend you visit the highest point
because the view takes in all quarters,
anywhere you concentrate
you'll be rewarded

even the tombs of the warriors
who fought for the freedom of the many
can be glimpsed
on the horizon

(the sunset echoing their blood)

the grave where you make offerings
to beings higher than we encounter down below
hidden
between a mound of ice and an old pine
near the path winding 'round boulders."

Ambling along unaware of strange surroundings
cloud cover grew deeper and evening dimmer

foolishly I had brought no lamp

only the last tune of a blackbird,
the first of a thousand drops
and the presage of cold wind to keep me company

56: WAYFARER

no use feeling for signposts . . .

footsteps . . .

a light growing gradually brighter . . .

a solitary lady holding a torch:

"Of course,
I'll help you find your way

the moon can be obscured for a long time
in these parts."

I shan't ask too much of the innkeeper

he seems at his wits end with overwork

the bed, though, is clean, the meal adequate
and a red flower
has been placed on my pillow

but I could do with a wash

dare I ask him to prepare a bath
to soak my tired limbs?

No,
I can hear him arguing with the maid.

The shutters are closed,
the curtains drawn
and lingering rain passes overhead

I'll finish the map,
repack my pack and rest
until smoke rises for the morning cup
of tea, sugar is sprinkled on fruit,
the latch key opens the outer door

until I take to the road again.

57

Transcendence

Similar to the wind,
I don't know from where it comes
or where it goes:

"Your moment is spent.
Your time has happened."

What if
I were to sew wings on my back,
leap from the cliff
and on warm air lift into the clouds?

I could wash my feet
with light, brush my cheeks
with rain yet to fall
and rinse my forehead in white.

It enters with conviction
and ascends with the same speed it approached:

"You could lie in a flower bed, reach into the blooms,
sprinkle nectar on an iris

57: TRANSCENDENCE

the broken stem could knit
and new growth rise unencumbered above vacant land."

What of the pollen that lodges on my skin?
Will it find new stigma,
bud again
on the same dark planet?

"In the hours left
you could let the colors open
where the sun brightens their hue."

Camelia leaves:

The fly on a blanched patch

it could be me, looking for somewhere
to lay my eggs
and leave them to take care of themselves.

How he came by
when my feelers stroked air before his head,
eyes made out the blur in his wake

the dry meat odor I gave off—

an invitation to find his way under my skin
and bring forth a new brood

succulent,
distended
and permeated with heat

as I foresaw
when he picked out my flight
from the rest.

Moisten the back of your hand and feel
from which direction the breeze emanates

inside the pulse
in your veins:

"You are the one I love."

Morning glory:

How he expected me to listen
when he talked,
hold no grudges if he demeaned me
in front of onlookers,
readily accept his criticism
even though I was guilty of naught

for he delved beneath the ordinary
and superfluous, surpassed the mundane
and trivial

had a right
to subsume every view to his purview,
every outlook to his overarching sensibility.

Despite the northern wind's bitter arrival,
inhale nut dry languor emanating from the south:

"In the eternal shadow I bloomed like a transparent sunflower."

Calendula:

The noisome mass washed up on the beach
at high tide,
crab shells
and kelp washed back again
when an exhausted scrounger stopped his search
for a swollen bud under the mess.

Order your physique
so your lungs breathe spent air into woodland,
your toes dig into grit
and your heart beats
with the sparrows bobbing to find a tidbit,
mosquito's whizzing toward fresh water
and the helianthus unfurling toward the source
of desire that wants it to live:

"The dove's surreptitious flight into dreamland—
your home,
the dew's unfettered formation
on a stalk–your destiny,

57: TRANSCENDENCE

the vacillating dance
of a bee indicating the path to follow—
your way."

Laburnum:

How he drank pints of rice wine,
didn't come home until early morning
when cats were clawing at each other's backs,
upended his meal
and acted out the worm chewing uncultivated soil

fastened a halter to my neck,
wrenched it this way and that

under broken streetlights dragged me where he willed.

Warm an insignia ring in tired hands
and throw it into the dust:

"I can whiten the shadow while you sleep at night."

Amaryllis:

How he,
venturing no further
than blood behind his eye
or the taste of burnt flesh under his breast,
shut the door in my face, took up my belongings
and tossed them in the street:

57: TRANSCENDENCE

"I have no need
for devotion."

Resonant
as a songbird with the uplift of vitality
from the earth meeting the furthest reach
of Heaven's descent
into the turmoil,
address white clouds with the certainty
that the world will endure beyond this year's calamities
and pitfalls:

"The sun ignited in my presence."

Violet:

How he would,
with the conviction of the already disembodied,
relinquish the musk and ripeness,
watch on
without having to involve his senses
in growth and rebirth

for,
imminent as tomorrow,
just outside his vison,
the lucent stretch rendered the promise
of fragility untainted by a mar
held in cupped hands
and warmed by a downdraft
from colorless lips.

57: TRANSCENDENCE

Blow gently on dandelion fluff

each seed will dissolve in rain:

"From solar traps for the unwary
I'll find no hesitation in beckoning a luminary
to a cliff jutting into the sea
and waves crashing into the base."

Lavender:

His wont to personify the ground
with droplets from his shadow,
entwine roots with the life sucking vine,
withstand the encroachment
of wrinkled lips
and parchment skin

eschew the incoming tide over his head.

Under a fresh breeze
and scented insides turning outwards,
taste iron flecks
and inhale like you were breathing from within her lungs:

"I'll never depart
nor blow into oblivion."

58
Happiness

I'll wear my best set
of clothes, comb my hair and wash my features

no one will suspect I don't belong.

I'll quote only the profoundest passages
from ancient sources,
tell of the deeds of heroes bent on survival,
augment discussion
with notions
of unsurpassed sincerity

anyone who listens
will believe I am trained to hold an audience in suspense.

When they serve dinner,
I'll take care not to slurp my soup,
spill beans on my napkin
or let loose
with noises that suit a lonely man
when he thinks no one is about

58: HAPPINESS

I'll be taken
for a gentleman.

When someone asks me what I do,
I'll refrain
from admitting the truth

I lie around in bed a lot of the day,
refuse to sweep the cobwebs under the eaves
and swat flies for pleasure

answer,
with focus on the lines I jotted down yesterday,
I work at creating a new vision
for humanity

somehow, with the effort I put into things,
streetlights will grow a little brighter,
rain pass by without wetting foundations,
obedience to higher realms burst forth
in red droplets on a yellow sheet,
lemon scent
and sugar sweet tweets from a forest

no one will think I am deluded.

What if the music begins
and we are meant to choose a partner?

58: HAPPINESS

Anxious foreboding will not pervade the ritual
of selection,
there will be someone whose rhythm
and timing feels awkward as my own.

We'll rise to the occasion

dance
onto the floor with hearts extended,
seek light beyond our dreams

in step with the beat
that makes the room shudder,
floorboards lift

the whirl concentrated in deference to the melody

aim at non-stopping until exhaustion

I'll be one with the crowd.

When the oration representing everything the organization wants to hear
about extraordinary flights surpassing its original intention
ends with smoke curling toward the ceiling,
I'll applaud
with the others

58: HAPPINESS

even though the ticket
was given me
by a salesman who passed by
on the off chance,
who couldn't make it

who thought I could do with a good night out.

59

Commiseration

The attack wasn't carried out by an armed thug
but the youth who delivered milk. He met up
with unsavory characters who led him astray.
So the barber said when he shaved my head. "What good
to pay taxes when nothing is done to lower crime?
Why put up with gangs hanging around the streets? Our home
isn't ours anymore." And undoubtedly he charged too high.

Outside the wind lifts the leaves
and litter skips along the road.

I would never distress an old woman
because I thought my need greater than her right
to keep what she earned. I hate thieves
who take more from life than what they put in,
dog droppings and the coarse minded

too lazy to put rubbish in a container,
unable to hold a child tenderly
or listen to guidance away from harm

that can't keep their noise down
when everyone is asleep.

59: COMMISERATION

"Always on the lookout
for weakness."

A gust bends foliage over an abandoned shrine.

Not that they'd care to use it.

Higher fields
where fruit is abundant
abandoned to "happiness",
compassion smeared with grey matter:

"Like a bucket of water without salt,
longing for otherworldliness
that never accomplishes anything
other than escape from worldly activity."

A grey limb looks as if it will break off
at any moment.

If a few coins dropped in my lap,
I would restore this sanctuary,
flood it with incense,
name it anew.

"Nothing to offer. All that blather—
nonsense.
Repose in serenity at the end of it all?
Take as much as the world can divulge,
alter the facts to suit your purpose,
live in a mansion."

59: COMMISERATION

Against the force
of the wind I close the door.

In shadows of a missing altar,
I'll lift sentiments above the planets,
intoxicate the Heavens with need
for rejuvenation.

"Days and years will end in absence
and a moist lip molded in stone."

Rain spatters the windows.

In imitation
of a nurse that lost a patient,
if I could change one thing,
I would listen more carefully
when he was admitted into my care.

"Embroil the many
in the far-flung paradise of an individual,
encounter demonic cries
for release with the same tone
and weight
of anger?"

A cord where the lamp used to hang swings to
and fro.

59: COMMISERATION

Light
is found in night-time sojourns,
love in giving the self-same visitation
and the expanse behind the sun.

"An outer-luminary will leave flaming orbs
and regain footing on harder ground."

An anxious parent tucks their child firmly in bed,
empty streets pronounce the dread of being caught outside.

I am not the vernal pasture
on a spring afternoon,
can't guide you beyond the stars

I belong with a passer-by who stamps her feet
when a pilferer lifts an heirloom,
wags a finger at an owner for failing to clean up

trusts they will be spared drawing blood
from a neighbor's heart
as the source of the droplets are beyond our reach.

60

A Way Nonetheless

With no motive than to while the time away
I call in on a meeting and hear words
to the effect
that a priest's eye should be purified
of malcontent and shaped like an almond.

At the end of the street
a self-made prophet enlightens a few standing to the side:

"Every action should resonate
with an ancient text

yet,
exceeded by harmony
and respect
of all whatever their origin."

An elderly gentleman with an ivory cane
can be heard to declare:

"Children should obey

no adventure, excitement
or frivolity

determination to keep the same tradition over millennia."

Holy men
swathed in robes kneel under an oak:

"We can no longer accept alternatives to our view

ultimately, the path will blaze through disbelief

God should never have a human face

a seeker,
however,
turn to the west and refuse to display an image."

A visitor to my door admonishes me
for not having listened to the everlasting word
meant to be the fount
of all that transcends ignorance.

In the news reports,
out of the mouths of soothsayers,
in temples where wanderers from another land congregate
and from friends who have long deliberated
on a power that transforms an open wound
into a sheltered cove:

60: A WAY NONETHELESS

"What use to invoke spirits
to accomplish the work
that could be done with a kind heart and a steady eye
on the outcome
known through the fall
of dark and light lines."

Esoterica:

the moon streaked with blood,
dewdrops splashing on a lip,
becoming clear
in an instant
and wiped away.

"Followers should rigidly adhere
to the rules
lest they are swallowed
by a demon,
a ghost will only appear to a bereaved partner
if the shutters are drawn and the light extinguished.

A believer can never think the planets are alive
or the sun a great being
aware of its destiny

what science tells us."

"Only in surrender to the belief that God is indwelling
and every consideration purporting to address the cosmos
other than with prayer abandoned
will the one who surpasses all opposites approach

60: A WAY NONETHELESS

when an arcane text is interpreted by a master,
the right invocation expressed
and the color of the candle meets Heavens aura
when it descends into the heart
can we accept someone who eats red meat,
finds the spice in our food too rich
and traces the path of skittles and balls."

At the end of the day I'll throw the coins
and ask whether it is appropriate to follow
when the blood-stained cross is lifted above the citadel
on the outskirts of the desert,
read the ancient texts to see if I shall come again
as a superior being who'd transform baser material
into a substance glowing with love,
address the guru emboldened with the certainty
he has descended from the heights beyond pain
with the same respect I would reserve
for a monk who traipsed from village to village
with a begging bowl and a poem in his heart.

Where a hymn rises
in appreciation for her devotion
and suffering,
I shall join in unabashedly

when the chant reaches a crescendo acclaiming his sovereignty,
I will bow
in obedience

60: A WAY NONETHELESS

when the man who has no creed
assumes that the only thing that matters
is his survival in comfort
I shall sit by him
and remark
on how nourishing his beef stew tastes.

61
Sincerity

If the wind was from the right quarter
I could acclimatize with great schemes,
address higher issues, understand the importance
of sacrificing time, effort and vitality,
determined to succeed where others have failed

yet still suffer the consequences of defeat

for I am capable
only of minor achievements,
of accomplishing little when I lay out
what my actual faculties
have in their power to effect.

I haven't wings
to fly into starlight,
but can imagine the actors who have descended
illuminated
by inner brightness

am unable to transform sensitivity into long-sightedness,
but am aware of the hidden tongue
that wakes me in the night:

61: SINCERITY

"I am

even though every inch
of soil is covered with frost, air
is thick
with mist and the temple's hidden from view

where you are."

I'll make my way
to the silence in the center:

"You are

despite the pendant gathering dust under the bed,
reminding of a relationship long ago,
the mirror reflecting wisps
of grey,
lips blackened
by sucking at ink brushes
and barely opened lids,
polished on a daily basis

where I am."

When I suspect someone has stolen the book
I treasure, read it through
and secreted it where it can't be read again,
I'll not raise my ire or curse the fiend
who deprived me, but recollect the empathy therein
that inspired me:

61: SINCERITY

passages which may,
with the tenderness born for the author
who evokes a furnace
between the blind minstrel craving another drop
and the prettiest widow
who'd always condescend
to give from the store she keeps unlocked
a mouthful,
melt the desire to break open another window,
reach in
and grab anything that may be sold
for a penny or two at the local fair.

Although I cannot reach the high point
of aspiration and claim heroic potency,
I am still capable of keeping up a polite demeanor,
of saying,
"no," when my internal sense
has no affinity
with what is offered,
"yes,"
when I know the love escaping from my heart
will make another smile

"I'm terribly sorry,"
when the moonlight surrendered from my grasp
has fallen on someone's face.

62

Hopelessness

Damp penetrates, the roof leaks
and leaves a stain.

I rearrange the furniture,
no temporary fix can keep out the drip

squeeze into the corner,
neck sore from holding my head
where the sunset provides lingering contrast

train my eye on levels transcending daybreak,
a red glow ruining a thorn's incarnation
into a newly formed petal

melt verdigris on an idol and paint the moon,
distance from repletion expanding with every tint
of mortality

out of the sheen,
isolate an acute cry splitting ice,
waking reluctant embodiment
out of slumber

62: HOPELESSNESS

study a drop splashing on the table,
an absent heart pumping in the silence

convey the sorrow
on hearing the loss my old friend endured
when his youngest fell from the swing,
a small card inscribed with,
"the deepest sympathy"

flesh and blood preceded by a word of kindness:

"I want you to know
I can never say anything
to compensate"

stumps outside cracking with cold.

The chill wind will follow leaves to the planet's end,
blare away at an out of focus moon
and moisten cheeks

the witless acts,
careless, throw away things said . . .

the stone lodged in my shin, forgotten.

62: HOPELESSNESS

I'll warm my left ear,
pick lint from your black suit
and steer you between the blooms laid out
on the pathway.

My lips will open
when the time is ready,
moments having accomplished something special resurface

a runny nose,
broken tooth
and swear words preferable.

Lonely as a shower in winter,
deep as midnight with the cat asleep,
close to the bruise above my knee,
I blow out the candle and go to bed.

63

An Uncertain Future

A few nights ago
when silence subdued the murmur in the shadows,
candlelight lit up an ornament on the mantle:

a fledgling poet
who lay on his back
and contemplated the peak
he'd just descended.

With the breeze swirling in his tracks,
he would have wandered many miles,
always questioning his identity:

"Who am I?
Where do I belong?
Will the journey reach a haven?"

He could have persevered
in a job purchasing bricks
for the construction of a new factory,
but with every order
he'd write another line and add it to the others
on in his desk:

63: AN UNCERTAIN FUTURE

"concrete slabs
and rust

I'll fit in with the others,
attentive to their pressure
until I crack."

"Yes," he exclaimed,
"in deference to the lost,
I'll take holy orders,
burn a candle at the end of the day,
study several manuals
with the intention of ministering to the sick."

However,
when light in every room
extinguished from a fault
and Heaven illuminated the way out,
"Follow me,
I can see the outlines of the citadel,
the morning star above its battlements,"
he'd linger:

"moonlight
on the pond,
the priest's taken off his robes,
bittersweet melon" . . .

in the glow a newborn finds on opening her lids,
shove his beak
into the fruit the farmer was unable to sell
at the market:

63: AN UNCERTAIN FUTURE

"a follicle sprouting no further
than a blemish,
the root embedded in the coldest hour before sunrise,
lifelong loneliness."

"I'll stay here
for ages

there's water to drink,
a bird's brain provides a nice place to rest:

shadow
on the water,
yellow fruit and soft insides,
an arrow from a warmer clime

tap, tap, tap
when I am not meant to remain here.

I'll ascend
with the full extent of my wing's spread
where planets converge in a speck
and immortals gather to hear waters babble,
mortals language of the clouds

merely delight in the undelighting:

63: AN UNCERTAIN FUTURE

light to shine on my back,
air to inhale through sunrise

claws that cling to a branch,
a length
of twine cutting into my neck

hung on a fence.

Further than pain
no one cares whether you enter or leave."

Deeply committed to preserving the one treasure I possess,
I built a structure to hold my books
and display my precious item

steeped in admiration,
when every step he had taken fell in with my own,
the glow on his forehead met the glow in my chest
and I felt I could recollect everything he endured,
the shelf gave way

later,
when I could bring myself to bear it,
I glued the broken pieces together,
tightened the screws,
hammered the nails a little deeper,
but stood in the clear

63: AN UNCERTAIN FUTURE

I could have made a mistake,
and my effort
at first glance
on the whole secure
weaken at the joints

collapse on the floor.

64
Almost There

By now
I should have brought to completion
the work I have been working on:

love-sick little bird flapping at windows
at two o'clock in the morning

underbelly pink
as insides brought to light,
lemon scent above a lobe,
boiling in fug above her thighs.

With no compulsion,
wondering why you chose
for a wet afternoon
to walk
thoroughly drenched
than listen to my song:

eye shadow,
drops
of spittle and rouge

64: ALMOST THERE

why you'd prefer to calm a crying orphan
than hold up the dilapidated building
which would serve as our future dwelling.

Out of nowhere,
wind lifts the veranda,
an acorn drops on the roof
and my neighbor rattles the doorhandle:

"Is it another hurricane?"

Not to blame innumerable interruptions,
I have an inkling
something is always out of my grasp:

lymph
and corpuscles steaming on ice,
liver paste bubbling on snow.

"What is it now?"

"I'm sorry
to bother you.

My windows are broken,
can you put me up for the night?"

"As long as you go
when things quieten."

64: ALMOST THERE

Fingers splay before a wounded eye,
throat murmurs simplify with echoes from the first born:

"A scarf around a thin throat keeps out the cold,
layers of fur keep you in the air."

Black light
will irradiate gentle space
where I could live forever,
moist riffles augment her pulse
and reach the blossom shedding tears
from a forbidden garden:

"Not even you can speckle columns with fragrant drops
from ethereal atmosphere."

I'll moisten a beak in hard water
and dislocate stubborn rocks,
find a way
that won't forbid entry
to where I am not wanted

when crimson ribbons dissolve,
lights flickering on
and off at random
glow intently on plumage,
swim in your veins,
dry feathers
in your warmth,
flutter on the horizon extending to Mars

64: ALMOST THERE

in other words,
I am not sure what lies under your skin,
but with one brusque remark, a caress?

I could enliven the thread joining Mercury
and frozen zones,
unearth a witness
before the earth evacuates under an ageing sun:

the magician
who'll make daylight appear
where night has opened a blind eye.

www.ingramcontent.com/pod-product-compliance
Lightning Source LLC
Chambersburg PA
CBHW071423150426
43191CB00008B/1025